DATE DUE

DEMCO

RECRUITING IN SPORTS

RECRUITING
IN
SPORTS

BY HANK NUWER

Franklin Watts 1989
New York London Toronto Sydney

Charts courtesy of Vantage Art, Inc.

Library of Congress Cataloging-in-Publication Data

Nuwer, Hank.
Recruiting in sports.

Bibliography: p.
Includes index.
Summary: Discusses the recruiting of high school
athletes for college sports teams.
1. College sports—United States. 2. Athletes—
United States—Recruiting. [1. Athletes—Recruiting.
2. College sports] I. Title
GV351.N89 1989   796'.071'173   89-9151
ISBN 0-531-10796-5

CONTENTS

RECRUITING IN SPORTS

INTRODUCTION

This book is intended primarily for high school athletes who want to participate in varsity athletics at the college level, particularly those who hope to receive financial assistance for participating. It is also an all-inclusive reference guide to help young athletes of both sexes cope with typical recruiting practices.

We will pull no punches when it comes to pointing out the evils of the recruiting system. At the same time, we will show the good that financial aid can do for athletes. Many a player has taken his or her scholarship and gone on to earn a degree, afterwards achieving dreams that otherwise might not have come true. This book does not condemn the system of recruiting. What it *does* condemn are the evils associated with recruiting. The reasoning behind this book, simply stated, is that if you're informed, you can better play the "recruiting game" than can those students who are uninformed or misinformed.

This inside look into the business of recruiting is intended to help players of all abilities who are interested in obtaining a scholarship based on athletic ability. Of course, this does not include NCAA Division III institutions which, at this writing (although there is always talk of new legislation), are prohibited from offering financial aid based on athletic skills. If you are a so-called blue-chip athlete—a superstar—there's a chapter for you. But if you happen to be an athlete who has lots of desire but average talent, this book is also for you. You'll learn how to attract a school's attention to get a scholarship or, if that's impossible, how to pursue alternatives to an athletic scholarship that can financially assist you while you try to make a school team as a walk-on.

Although this book is of particular value for football and basketball players, it can be read with interest by any athlete. Much of the material, in addition, pertains to athletes of both sexes. The book tells why schools pursue some players while occasionally ignoring others of equal or greater talent. It also addresses the special problems of the high school athlete who is trying to decide whether to turn professional immediately or attend a college or university first.

Divided into chapters that treat the major and minor decisions that student-athletes face during their high school years, the book also contains advice and observations from athletes and coaches. Many of these men and women were interviewed specifically for this book; others were interviewed on the subject of recruiting for articles that the author wrote as contributing writer with *Inside Sports* and as a frequent contributor to *Sport* and other national magazines. Also interviewed were members of the media and the National Collegiate Athletic Association (NCAA). Finally, the NCAA's own literature was carefully perused, in order to translate its do's and don'ts into language that can be understood easily by any high school student.

The decision to pursue a college degree while competing in organized sports is the first major commitment many young people must make. Unfortunately, too many athletes in the past have relied on friends, relatives, coaches, or—Heaven forbid!—a recruiter to do their thinking for them. Many have learned—too late—that not even veteran high school coaches or the most well-intentioned advisers know enough about this complicated subject to give wise recommendations. By reading about the good and bad experiences that other athletes have had, readers can learn how to solve recruiting dilemmas as they crop up.

Above all, this book should help to demystify the practice of recruiting. And once you understand how the system works, you can deal with it in a sensible, businesslike manner, actually using it to your advantage. You'll also rest easier knowing that you have used all available information to make a decision that most likely will influence you the rest of your life.

It is also the hope of the author of this book that the discussions included may indirectly help stem some of the more flagrant abuses of recruiting. If athletes—particularly so-called blue-chippers—give those recruiters who are charlatans and glorified gangsters a boot out the door instead of a signature on the dotted line, the illegal and unethical practices can and will stop.

As author, I have an additional, more personal, reason for writing this book. I have two sons. One of them, Christian, is a high school football tight end and pole-vaulter at Huron High School in Ann Arbor, Michigan. He is seeking a college scholarship even as I write these words. And someday my younger son, Adam, might also follow in his brother's cleatprints. Therefore, I am writing this book as a labor of love to help out my boys, but it gives me great satisfaction to know that someone else's son or daughter may also benefit from my research.

1

THE BUSINESS OF RECRUITING

Recruiting is not unusual in the academic world. Colleges not only search for talented athletes to stock their teams; they also compete for students with the potential to become scientists, engineers, and computer whizzes. In addition to recruiting students, university presidents and deans vie to obtain the best coaches and faculty members, occasionally even raiding rival schools in the process of trying to land the best catches. Several Texas universities have waged successful campaigns to lure Nobel Prize winners to their Lone Star campuses. It is not unusual for top-notch universities to build made-to-order laboratories to attract scientists with national reputations. The best and brightest faculty in all disciplines vie with each other to obtain endowed chairs. These chairs are sponsored by an individual or a corporation, and those who have them make far more in salary than their less talented or less lucky colleagues make.

Nor is recruiting limited to college campuses. The big computer companies and other businesses pay "headhunters" large sums to steal qualified men and women away from the competition. The armed forces have long known the value of recruiting to obtain qualified men and women. And even body shops and beauty parlors try to pry loose skilled helpers from rivals across town.

As any blue-chip athlete and his or her parents can testify, recruiting can be a terribly frustrating and stressful experience. Even for the mediocre athlete, competing with the half-million juniors and seniors playing high school football each year, the task of getting at least one coach to notice his or her talents and to offer a scholarship can be quite frustrating.

For the superstar high school athlete, it is a time when the ego soars. For the marginal player, it is time to apply for Division II or even Division III schools to gain playing time, or to take a long shot and try to make a top team as a walk-on.

This book is intended primarily for those high school students who have at least an outside chance of getting a scholarship to play college ball. Ironically, those students who are being pursued by colleges are often as confused as those who aren't.

Recruiting is a stressful time not only for athletes and parents but also for college coaches. Coaches recruit full-time for about three months each year and part-time for the rest of the year. No coach—no matter how persuasive or how much a winner—can sign every recruit. Worse, whether a coach is happy with a recruiting class or not, sportswriters will rank each recruiting class and report in the paper how the team is doing before it has had a chance to get itself organized. University of Michigan football coach Bo Schembechler maintains that "it takes two years to find out how you really did,"[1] but try telling that to disappointed fans. The headlines when a top-rated blue-chipper is signed are almost as big as the ones accorded an important victory—particularly in states such as Texas and

Florida, which fight so hard to attract the best resident athletes.

What is it like to be heavily recruited? Picture yourself with sixty coaches, assistant coaches, and alumni of various schools all wanting not just a piece of you but every ounce of you for the next four or five years that you're in college. Some recruiters take a motel room in the hometown of a major blue-chip athlete, staying anywhere from a few days to several months in hopes of impressing or wearing down the target of their campaign with their persistence.

Imagine your phone ringing at all hours—even after midnight and before 6 A.M.—with recruiters on the line "just to keep in touch." Recruiting has driven more than one person crazy. It can and does disrupt family life, studies, a parent's business, and the recruit's social life. If you think about it, you'll understand why recruits often give oral commitments or sign letters of intent just to stop all the hounding. Usually, these recruits regret the hastiness of their decision as soon as the victorious recruiter leaves the area.

All the fuss of the recruiting process ends right after National Signing Day. Once the player and parents put their signatures on the dotted lines—the signing being prominently noted in the hometown paper's sports section—all the attention suddenly stops. The recruit becomes just another college athlete, and the coach often assumes a far different personality, turning from kindly uncle to drill sergeant. However, unlike other students, recruited athletes often feel that their lives belong to the National Collegiate Athletic Association (NCAA) and to the public, not to themselves.

"Pressure . . . carries over into athletes' lives off-the-floor," basketball player Andrew Kennedy told *The Sporting News* when he was with the University of Virginia.

"Their every move is scrutinized under an electron microscope, and their lives become somewhat abnormal."[2]

Colleges spend small fortunes on recruiting. For example, until the NCAA banned the practice of allowing use of more than one color in the media guides put out by all big-time athletic departments, schools such as Louisville, Kansas, and Iowa State printed glossy, full-color guides that doubled as recruiting tools to send to athletes. The University of Kentucky alone spends $13.5 million a year on its athletic programs. North Carolina State spends $11 million. It's typical for a university to spend more than $300,000 a year on recruiting expenses, including travel, the printing of brochures, coaching clinics, and game films.

"If disaster struck and you had to cut everything out of your budget, the last two things you would cut are recruiting and salaries," maintains Vince Dooley, a former Georgia head football coach. "If you cut those two you have no program. That's how important recruiting money is."[3]

Individual scholarships vary greatly from one college to another, but there's no question that they are as good as gold to today's high school seniors. By way of example, one football scholarship (including room and board) awarded by Southern Methodist University costs the university roughly $15,000. Multiply that cost by ninety-five allowable scholarships, and SMU's total scholarship bill for football alone is approximately $1.7 million.

Money is the name of the recruiting game. When a team wins a national championship in a major sport, applications to that school swell. Winning seasons make alumni checkbooks open wider. After winning a national championship in football, Penn State received a record $48.8 million in donations compared to $37.6 million the previous year. "We think the Nittany Lions' 1986 national title probably helped us in that it heightened the awareness of our needs with our alumni," Dave Gearhart, vice-president for development and university relations, told *The Sporting News.* Alumni also feel particularly generous when players from their college turn professional.

In addition, profits from postseason play significantly fatten up a university's revenues, as well as those of Division I conferences. For example, Final Four college basketball teams now receive more than $1 million each (even teams eliminated in the first round earn $280,000), and the tournament itself generates $29 million. Football bowls also provide healthy payoffs, including $2.2 million for the Sugar Bowl winner and nearly that much for the Sunkist Fiesta Bowl. In 1986, colleges that participated in bowl games received $47 million.

But although individual athletes help money flow into the college's coffers—and a Heisman candidate alone can fill stadiums with fans—the National Collegiate Athletic Association (NCAA) has steadfastly refused to allow colleges to pay most athletes. The NCAA, an organization whose function is to administer the policies and rules that its membership votes to adopt, seems to have the best intentions but often hurts individual athletes with its blanket policies. By not paying athletes, men and women from financially strapped families are at a disadvantage. Athletes currently can accept no more than $1,400 in federal Pell Grant monies, while non-athletes are eligible for up to $2,100. The only athletes allowed to accept money for competing in college competitions, partially because their personal expenses tend to be high, are college rodeo contestants, who get paid cash for winning their events. Ironically, college rodeo performers, however, have more-stringent academic standards than do their basketball-and football-playing counterparts. The National Intercollegiate Rodeo Association—the sport's governing body—insists that competitors maintain a minimum grade point average of 2.0.

Will athletes someday be paid to play? Many respected coaches think the day is long overdue. Sonny Smith, Auburn's basketball coach, maintains student-athletes should get something, even if only a small amount. Joe Paterno, head football coach at Penn State, agrees.

"I've been criticized because a lot of people think it's inconsistent with my ideals that I think we ought to pay players or give them a certain amount of spending money," says Paterno. "But back in about 1955 or '56, we used to give the kids $15 a month for spending money. We gave them room, board, books and tuition—the same thing we have now—plus $15 for spending money. An economist went through the process of figuring what $15 would be worth today, and it's worth $65 a month now in spending money."[4]

Paterno believes that the most common form of player cheating—the taking of small amounts of cash from boosters, or friends of the university,—might be alleviated if the old practice of giving spending money were reinstated. "You take a kid in college today who's dirt-poor—he simply has no dignity," says Paterno. "He can't pick up a check. He can't buy a shirt he likes. He can't go to the movies. We make kids wear coats and ties on our trips. Some kids who come to us don't have a coat. They have to go home, make some money, and buy a coat.

"There are great temptations for somebody out of the mainstream. He'd be tempted by somebody who'd say, 'I want you to be able to join a fraternity—here's a hundred bucks.' And a kid takes it. Or somebody says, 'Get a decent shirt,' and the kid shoplifts. We ought to be fair to the kid. I don't think that's paying him; that's giving him a legitimate scholarship, because we do that in so many other areas. The whole college experience should be meaningful—not just going to classrooms—but you've got to be in the mainstream. You can't be in the mainstream if you don't have a $10 bill in your pocket once in a while."

There seems to be some additional support for paying athletes to play. In Nebraska in 1988, state senator Ernie Chambers of Omaha sponsored a bill (vetoed by Governor Kay Orr, but sponsors promised to reintroduce it next session) that said that exploitation of football players by colleges must stop and that monetary compensation should be given athletes for the entertainment they provide. "Everything they do meets the definition of a job," said Senator Chambers.[5]

Until the NCAA allows athletes to play for pay, abuses may continue to occur, but the recruit must stand tall and resist attempts at corruption even if others succumb to it. Even when head coaches themselves are beyond reproach, the system often breaks down when assistant coaches or boosters take it upon themselves to try to insure winning at any cost.

Assistant coaches can be disciplined or fired in extreme cases, but boosters are difficult to control. Oklahoma football coach Barry Switzer told *The Sporting News* that he was "not so naive to think that boosters might not do favors for players."[6] The Indianapolis Colts running back Eric Dickerson told a Houston television station that before he signed with Southern Methodist University, boosters from Texas, Texas A & M, and Arkansas offered him "anything that caught your attention," including automobiles, illegal payments, and women. And Dick Lowe, a Texas Christian University booster, whom *The Sporting News* called "a key money man in the scandals at the Fort Worth school," claimed that Southwestern Conference running backs received an automobile, $1,000 a month, and a $10,000-to-$25,000 bonus for signing a letter of intent. All this seems particularly jarring when you consider that many assistant professors of English, despite their Ph.D. degree, receive annual starting salaries under $20,000.

It may take legal action to stop booster improprieties. An angry Southern Methodist alumnus, Representative John Bryant, a Texas Democrat, introduced a bill in Washington that called for a prison sentence for boosters who act illegally. The bill would also deprive universities of federal funds when they tolerate such unethical conduct. On the state level, another Texas Democrat, state senator John Montford, wants the Texas legislature to allow colleges to sue unethical boosters for up to $10,000 plus damages for loss of TV and bowl revenue.[7]

Another way to end collegiate cheating is for recruits to realize that their own integrity has been questioned when someone offers illegal inducements. Rather than feel flattered, they should feel insulted when a booster or coach sizes them up as men or women who can be bought as long as the price is right. And because the NCAA special convention voted 436 to 0 in 1985 to hold student-athletes accountable for violations of NCAA rules, it's only a matter of time before recruits who go around with open hands looking for illegal handouts receive exactly what they deserve—ineligibility for one or more years. Before this, only an institution was punished for NCAA transgressions, while an equally guilty player got away without penalties. Consider Sean Stopperich, the SMU recruit who received $11,000 in improper cash and perks from Mustang boosters and who was an important factor in the school's being given the so-called death penalty in 1987. (An institution that is judged a "repeat" offender by the NCAA— that is, a school found guilty of a second major violation within five years of a prior major penalty—is subject to the harshest possible penalties. The most severe sanctions are these: the prohibition of all intercollegiate competition in the sport involved for one or two seasons, the suspension of all involved coaches from coaching activities for two years, and the elimination of additional athletic scholarships and recruiting activities in the sport involved for two years.) Stopperich then went to Temple University on another scholarship, where President Peter Liacouras foolishly said, "We're very proud that a person like Sean chose Temple."[8]

Recruits must realize that schools and coaches who offer illegal inducements should be treated with the disrespect they deserve. But all too often, players have been just as willing to act unethically as their elders. The situation at Southern Methodist University during the last decade was so bad that two SMU football players even broke into an athletic administrator's desk and stole the payroll for the month in order to get the money illegally promised to them. The players were caught but boldly refused to give the money back, knowing that the coaches were in no position to prosecute. According to the report of the United Methodist Church Bishops' Committee, which investigated the SMU scandal, "The payroll money was replaced by the booster who supplied it."[9]

Not all coaches are cheaters, of course. More than one has registered disgust at the improprieties in recruiting that have become commonplace. Coach Bob Knight of Indiana not only resigned but removed himself as president of the National Association of Basketball Coaches to protest rampant violations. "I'm through sitting next to people who talk sanctimoniously about our business, then go out and break the rules," Knight told the *San Diego Tribune.* "Earlier this year [1986], I got a letter from an administrator at Illinois, complaining about my referring to their athletic program as a 'mess.' In my reply, I pointed out that in the 12 years I've been at Indiana, they've been on probation four times and [have] been investigated on three other occasions. 'If there's a better word in the English language than "mess" to describe that situation,' I wrote, 'please advise me as to what it is and I'll use it. Instead of scolding me, why don't you apologize to the rest of us for cheating?' " Concluded Knight, "I'm still waiting to hear back from him." [10]

Knight is not the only one suspicious of his peers. According to a survey conducted by Denver's *Rocky Mountain News* in August 1988, "a group comprising nearly half of all major coaches believes one in every five big-school programs cheats to gain an edge."

When the Reverend Theodore M. Hesburgh retired as president of Notre Dame, he delivered a parting shot against cheaters, saying that the Fighting Irish no longer wanted to play them. "We're not going to play the schools that are constantly on probation," said Hesburgh. "We've lost $500,000 the last two years because we couldn't televise a game against a team on probation. . . . Why should we be penalized because the other school is on probation?" [11] Notre Dame basketball coach Digger Phelps agreed with that view and added an interesting twist of his own, suggesting that the government should stop giving tax breaks to colleges who fail to graduate at least 75 percent of their athletes on scholarship. [12]

Later in this book is a long list of schools that have run afoul of NCAA regulations in recent years. Recruits may wish to think twice before dealing with those institutions who are constantly in hot water with the NCAA. Even if some players are honest and don't take one dime improperly, they still suffer from a negative public image by being associated with an institution that cheats. Joe Paterno has an excellent philosophy that every recruit should remember when schools and coaches with a record of improper doings come calling. "We have a saying around [Penn

State]," says Paterno. "It isn't enough to *be* fair; you must *appear* to be fair. There's a big difference."

Another reason athletes must pay attention to what schools and coaches have done in the past involving rules violations is that no coach is going to come right out and admit that he or she consistently cheats. In fact, since coaches often tell athletes what they hope to hear, a dishonest coach may lie to an honest kid, saying that his or her school and program are clean. "The problem is not the good, self-assured coaches who are in control of their programs," said Frank Remington, chairman of the NCAA Committee on Infractions. "It's the guy on the bottom who is trying to work his way to the top. That's the guy who tends to say, 'I'm at a recruiting disadvantage, and if I'm going to survive I'm going to need an edge somewhere.' That edge, unfortunately, results in their doing some things they shouldn't do."[13]

Without question, the best hope of colleges to get their collective acts together is the NCAA. It is the only organization with enough clout to make member institutions behave. As Jerry Tarkanian's lawyer, Samuel Lionel, said when asked why Nevada–Las Vegas doesn't simply secede from the organization: "The NCAA is the only game in town." Although there have been rumblings from Penn State's Joe Paterno and other coaches about seceding from the organization, there is little chance a major college will leave. For one thing, scheduling non-NCAA teams would be impossible. Literally, there would be no one to play.

The NCAA's reputation among fans stems from its role as judge and jury in investigations of improprieties involving players, coaches, boosters, and colleges. Admittedly, the NCAA's watchdog role has been made more difficult by those who charge coaches with cheating without substantiating their accusations. "Coach [Bob] Knight claims he knows that certain schools are buying players, but when we interview him for hour after hour, he has no information," complains Frank Remington. "There's no basis for saying that proven winners or big schools are given a free pass. What we try to do is to be fair to everybody."

Another problem the NCAA faces is that, unlike a court of law, it has no subpoena power. "We have no way to insist that the student-athlete be there," said Frank Remington.

Few students are afraid of the NCAA; it can't send them to jail or fine them. As place-kicker Jeff Ward said when he was at the University of Texas, "It's not a legal organization. If I was ever to be questioned as far as breaking the rules, I think I'd just refuse to answer. I don't understand why more people don't do that."[14] But for every athlete that is cynical and uncooperative, there are others who are straightforward and willing to work with the NCAA.

The NCAA's greatest strength seems to be precisely what causes its weaknesses: The institution is a giant force to reckon with. What are its advantages? For one thing, the NCAA generates huge sums of money for member institutions by staging such events as the Final Four, the College World Series, and the football bowl games. Second, it also has done much to curb drug abuse, thereby improving the image of college sports (although admittedly the NCAA has sometimes invaded an athlete's right to privacy to accomplish its goal of drug-free amateur sports, and— perhaps unnecessarily—has made certain over-the-counter medicines illegal). Third, there are fewer cheaters in college sports as a result of investigations, and it truly would be frightening to imagine what lengths some coaches, boosters, and players would go to without the NCAA to deter them.

On the negative side, the NCAA has been so financially successful that there have been temptations for its employees. "I don't think the NCAA can handle [college athletics] anymore," William C. Friday, the former president of the University of North Carolina system told the *Atlanta Journal and Constitution.* "They make too much money for themselves now. It's the power of the dollar that no college administration has yet devised a way of controlling."

Proof that the NCAA has become big business in itself was provided by the *Washington Post,* which carefully documented the NCAA's hypocrisy in revealing that then–NCAA executive director Walter Byers renewed a $500,000 loan from the United Missouri Bank of Kansas City at an interest rate of 8 percent while other customers paid as high as 16.75 percent. Of course, the NCAA has had its own dealings with United Missouri. And in view of Byers's actions, can colleges who are on NCAA probation because their players took improper loans or gifts of cars from boosters be blamed for their actions?

Furthermore, critics think the NCAA is being two-faced when it prohibits players from taking payment as basketball extras in the movie *Hoosiers* or suspends former Indiana guard Steve Alford for posing (unpaid) for a sorority charity calendar, particularly when the NCAA then uses Alford and other players in antidrug or pro-NCAA spots that result in that organization's becoming even more of a giant. The NCAA, however, introduced legislation in January 1988 that allows athletes to pose for charities.

But on a brighter note, there is evidence that the new NCAA executive director, Richard D. Schultz, is attempting to make the organization more responsive to member needs. For one thing, the NCAA has finally simplified its official *Manual,* although it is still not fun to read. For another, individuals in the NCAA are showing more compassion toward "understandable" infractions, such as cases where a coach or booster has helped an athlete return home for a funeral or family emergency.

"I, for one, have thought you should give one, preferably two, round-trip paid airline tickets to the student from campus to home and back," says Frank Remington. "Many of the violations we see are with low-income athletes who are a long way from home. Coaches try to help with airfare and get into trouble."

Remington contends that the NCAA must put more emphasis on instituting the equivalent of "Neighborhood Crime Watches" to keep coaches and players from committing infractions.

"It's a lot like medicine's response to cancer," he concludes. "I think you can't cure it now, but that doesn't mean you shouldn't work on a cure. You can try, hopefully, to keep it under control. You try to deal with situations before they arise.

"I think pressures are so great that you can't completely eliminate violations, but we can assure the honest people that we are doing everything possible to ensure that cheating doesn't pay."

CHOOSING THE RIGHT SCHOOL

Broadcasting legend Howard Cosell, speaking at a Dickinson College sports symposium, declared that athletic departments must finally understand that the reason their athletes come to college is to get an education. "There is a crying need for every college president . . . to stand up and to say, 'We've had it—academics first and athletics second.' "[1]

Digger Phelps agrees, insisting that he feels a responsibility to graduate his athletes, saying that it comes down to "being Number One at any cost versus teaching young people the art of competition." Maintains Phelps, "College coaches who are concerned and college presidents need to put athletics in the right perspective so that youngsters can have balance in their lives. . . . The athletic department is a part of the college environment. . . . It works well here [at Notre Dame] because it's a two-way street. It's never been out of balance because I won't let the youngsters abuse [the system]. In fact, I have a rule here that if I find you cut class during the season, you don't play the next game. We really encourage them to be *student*-athletes."[2]

So upset by recruiting violations and the untoward place of athletics in society was former University of Chicago president Robert Maynard Hutchins, that he once labeled the athletic scholarship a fraud that takes advantage of American youth. Even though one of the all-time great football coaches, Amos Alonzo Stagg, had once coached at Chicago, President Hutchins permanently dissolved the football team because he insisted there was only one way to win—to cheat.

"We could subsidize players or encourage our alumni to do so," wrote Hutchins in the *1940 Essay Annual.* "There is no doubt that on the whole the game has been a major handicap to education in the United States. If you win you must keep on winning."

The problem of recruiting goes back to the early days of college sports. When the great football coach Fielding Yost arrived at the University of Michigan in 1901, he brought three athletes with him from the West Coast to be certain that his winning ways at Stanford University would continue in Ann Arbor. One of the athletes admitted that Yost promised him $1,500 to play. In his early years at Michigan, Yost—who was paid a higher salary than any professor at the institution—violated eligibility rules with impunity, and he coached long enough to become embarrassed whenever references to his recruiting violations were made. "All of us who have had Yost or any Yost-like men about are not to be counted as sinless," said David S. Jordan, Stanford's president.

Among other transgressions, Yost admitted at least one player (Joe Maddock) to Michigan with an undeserved graduate status, after the player had lied about graduating from Albion College. "The plain truth is that our Michigan [athletes] are professional," one disgruntled Michigan faculty member told *Collier's* magazine in a 1905 muckraking article.[3]

Eighty-two years after that article appeared, the football tail still wagged the academic dog. A shocking 1987 study by three Indiana University researchers found that nearly two-thirds of the 130 Division I programs they investigated made a practice of "clustering" their athletes in so-called Mickey Mouse disciplines to receive what *The Sporting News* blasted as "all-but-bogus" degrees. The researchers found that only 40 percent of NCAA Division I players earn a college degree, and that a high percentage of those who do graduate leave the premises with shaky credentials earned in "less rigorous" disciplines. "We're at a real disadvantage against competitors who admit near-illiterates," complained Notre Dame spokesman Father Edmund Joyce, whose school rejects the "clustering" concept as akin to academic fraud. "We're playing by another set of rules."[4]

Other schools play by less noble rules. When a coach such as University of Wyoming football coach Al Kincaid put emphasis on recruiting top student-athletes and graduating them, his school fired him for not winning enough games. Gary Cunningham, the Wyoming athletic director, tried to justify his firing of the coach by telling sports columnist Art Spander: "We were just not putting people in the stands. . . . People in the state . . . stopped supporting our program."

Spander, who refers to paid athletes as "mercenaries," told his readers: "In Wyoming, the state university exists not to develop doctors but to produce sellouts. . . . At Wyoming, the administration did not permit Kincaid to lose and survive. You survive by enrolling a halfback who can run 100 yards faster than he can write his name, by taking in a kid who is able to dribble between his legs, but who is unable to conjugate a verb."[5]

An assistant coach at Division I Northwestern who left to become head football coach at Division III Drake, which grants no scholarships under NCAA rules, said that he expected the change to be refreshing. "Division III is a wholesome world," said Coach Nick Quartaro. "People choose your program for all the good things college is about—academics, campus life and things like that."[6]

Another school that plays by a different rule book from Notre Dame's is the University of Miami, which allowed fourth-year junior Vinny Testaverde, then aiming for the Heisman Trophy, to take Introduction to Sports, Introduction to Recreation, and Sports Injury and Nutrition while taking the 'Canes to a 10–2 season in 1985. And after Testaverde was drafted by the Tampa Bay Buccaneers, he simply dropped out of school, providing a terrible role model for young men and women to follow.[7]

Art Rooney, a Pittsburgh Steelers vice-president, had this to say about the quality of education in America: "If you're in college five years, you should be able to read—but some guys [in pro football] can't read."[8] Things in college football have gotten so bad that one Southern Methodist booster, Jerry LeVias, told the *Dallas Times Herald* that he actually had paid athletes cash as "incentives to get [good] grades," convinced apparently that they wouldn't study on their own.

But there are some hopeful signs. In 1988, the College Football Association surveyed its member institutions and found that 50.3 percent of all boys recruited to play football in 1982 graduated, the highest percentage since the survey began in 1981. Since 1981, Notre Dame has won or tied for the honor of first place in the survey four times, while Duke won or tied three times and Virginia won twice. In 1988, Notre Dame reported that 100 percent of its 1982 recruiting class had graduated, while Duke, Virginia, and Penn State graduated 90 percent of their players.

Many schools reported that they graduated 70 percent

of their players. These institutions included Boston College, Georgia Tech, Kansas State, Maryland, Rice, Syracuse, Tulane, and Vanderbilt. Unfortunately, some of these graduate-players (at Maryland, for example) earned their degrees in less than rigorous disciplines, as defined by the Indiana University study.[9]

Moreover, a 1988 survey of football coaches revealed that most coaches (68 percent) dislike a recent practice instituted by the University of Pittsburgh and other schools that provides bonuses to coaches who graduate a high percentage of players. These coaches told *The Rocky Mountain News* that "helping athletes make progress toward their degree is a basic requirement of a coach's job, and a coach should not receive compensation for it." Typical of respondents was the University of Wisconsin's Don Morton, who declared, "I don't need a bonus to execute a basic responsibility of my position." Echoed Notre Dame's Lou Holtz, "Why get a bonus for doing a job the university hired you to do?"[10]

Notre Dame's basketball program also graduates close to 100 percent of its players, and Coach Digger Phelps places academics ahead of sports rather than the other way around. This is the norm at less sports-pressured institutions. "There's no place you can hide anyone here," says Phelps, noting that Notre Dame has no so-called Mickey Mouse majors to hide athletes. "The student-athlete's peer pressure here is going to be in favor of academics. The student-athlete's in an intellectual climate, looking . . . to find the right criteria . . . so you can pursue a degree to survive after basketball. I had an architect graduate here. It took him five years to do it, but it's a five-year program. Billy Hanzlik [1980 NBA first-round draft pick] was an engineering student and got a degree in engineering. I never saw him on Mondays because his labs weren't over until five o'clock. We don't start practices here until 4:30

P.M., because we want those kids taking the courses that they need."

But coaches can only do so much, and incoming freshmen must realize that they need to take increasing responsibility for the quality of the education they receive. As one survey of college athletes pointed out, all too many high school seniors choose the institution without giving much thought as to how their choice affects the rest of their lives. The survey demonstrated that athletes ranked "finding a job after graduation" fourteenth on a fourteen-point scale, behind such other factors as alumni influence, summer employment opportunities, and the win/loss record of the university.[11]

High school student-athletes must take the decision of which college to choose very seriously. Quite often, when a college athlete chooses the wrong school, the student eventually becomes unhappy, disgruntled, or homesick. In that case, the only choices are to stay and be miserable, drop out, or transfer to another institution, making yourself ineligible to play for one full year. Paul Glonek, a Palos Hills, Illinois, defensive tackle, has made all the wrong sort of headlines during his career. He signed with Notre Dame but could not meet that school's academic standards. He attended summer school at the University of Illinois, but rejected that school shortly before fall, choosing instead to play with the University of Iowa. But after Iowa suspended him for disciplinary reasons prior to the 1988 Holiday Bowl, he announced that he was again shopping for a school to attend.[12]

Another good case in point is that of an outstanding Philadelphia, Mississippi, running back named Marcus Dupree. Basically a small-town youth at heart, Dupree nonetheless chose the University of Oklahoma over a barrage of other offers and found himself in the glass fish tank that constitutes big-time Sooners football. The running back left the school amid much bad publicity about him and Oklahoma, and he never did fulfill expectations that he would one day be a player of the caliber of an O. J. Simpson. He had a brief, unmemorable fling in the pros before an injury ended his football career.

Players wind up attending the wrong colleges for many reasons. The weakest select schools because a friend or girlfriend selected that school. Others make the decision solely because the campus looked pretty in a brochure or publicity film. Some even choose a school because their athletic hero attended it, or they buckle under pressure from a parent or relative to attend the old alma mater. The corruptible or the poor sometimes choose a school because a recruiter or booster offered a car, sexual favors, or cash—illegal inducements that no ethical coach or institution would ever endorse. Others may take a coach's word that his or her institution is academically superior to other schools.

"A lot of coaches will lie to you and say their graduation rates are highest," charged Nevada–Las Vegas coach Jerry Tarkanian. "But coaches will tell you anything. You can't believe them."[13] Tarkanian should know. After all, a recent study by two UNLV professors demonstrated that many of his basketball players remained eligible only because physical-education professors awarded grades that were highly inflated compared to the grades their colleagues teaching other subjects awarded.

What is the right way to select a college? First of all, the student-athlete must take a long, careful look at his or her abilities, priorities, and needs. The best place, in the long run, is the institution that stresses the importance of a good education.

Student-athletes who choose football or basketball "factories" because they feel certain that a pro career is in the offing are foolish. Even blue-chip players need to have a backup plan for their lives in the all-too-possible event that a professional career becomes out of reach. Career-ending injuries in college are commonplace, for one thing. For another, there simply aren't that many opportunities. The Center for Sports and Society at Northeastern University estimates, for example, that the National Basketball Association has only forty-eight openings a year and 4,400 top-level college seniors to choose from. Moreover, even those who make the NBA have a less than 40 percent chance of hanging on as a player for three years.

The National Football League is equally difficult for players to break into following college. Even those who do join those hallowed ranks do so for an average of only 3.2 years. Worse, even athletes who do get to play in the pros suffer great emotional distress when their careers are over if they don't have a backup career. Utah Jazz player Bill Robinzine couldn't adjust to life without basketball and committed suicide. Terry Furlow, another former Jazz player, turned to drugs and was killed in an automobile accident.

You must take responsibility for your academic life from the time you begin to decide which college is the right choice for you. You must carefully read the catalogs and brochures all institutions of your choice publish. Bear in mind that universities spend considerable sums of money to print the most compelling literature they can send students. Don't be overly impressed by full-color photographs or expensive, glossy paper. Instead, pay attention to what's printed on the page.

First and foremost, is the school accredited? In other words, is it an academic program that future employers or prestigious graduate schools believe is worth something? What is "accreditation"? According to one professional association, "Accreditation means that a unit [school, college, department, division] has been evaluated and has passed a thorough examination by a team of educators, media and industry professionals. It also means that the school has undergone a penetrating self-study which emphasized attention to innovative educational and training techniques."

There are some other criteria beyond accreditation that should be considered by students hoping to enter certain demanding professions. One typical method of judging larger institutions is to find out whether the Carnegie Foundation for the Advancement of Teaching has classified the institution as a "research university of the First Class." There are only forty-five schools so designated in the country. Another way is to inquire whether the institution ranks among the Top 100 research universities in research funding as designated by the National Science Foundation (see Chart 1). Unfortunately, not all institutions that employ top researchers make them available to undergraduate students, and so even if a school is judged the best it doesn't always mean its teachers are the best. Chapter Six gives athletes some specific ways to judge the quality of a school's teaching that might not be apparent just by reading its printed materials.

What about the athlete's choice of a major? If undecided about a future career, a student may decide to wait a year or even longer to declare a major. One possibility is simply to enroll in so-called general studies or liberal arts courses and to take the college's basic required courses for a year or two without worrying about taking classes in a particular field.

However, if the student does decide to choose a major right away, he or she should find out if that field of study meets the approval of the U.S. Office of Education and/or the Council on Postsecondary Accreditation. Just as institutions can receive accreditation, so too can many departments. For example, Ball State University's Department of

CHART 1
FACT FILE: The Top 100 Institutions in Total
Research-and-Development Spending for Fiscal 1987

	U.S. funds for research & development		Total funds for research & development	
	Amount	Rank	Amount	Rank
Johns Hopkins U.*	$476,290,000	1	$510,896,000	1
Massachusetts Inst. of Technology † .	206,785,000	2	264,416,000	2
U. of Wisconsin, Madison	149,665,000	4	254,493,000	3
Cornell U. †	144,604,000	6	244,840,000	4
Stanford U. †	204,386,000	3	240,885,000	5
U. of Michigan	137,558,000	8	224,890,000	6
U. of Minnesota	109,003,000	15	222,381,000	7
Texas A&M U.	75,432,000	26	219,853,000	8
U. of California, Los Angeles	130,763,000	10	188,831,000	9
U. of Illinois, Urbana–Champaign ...	104,420,000	17	188,682,000	10
U. of Washington	145,184,000	5	187,062,000	11
U. of California, San Diego	142,751,000	7	183,047,000	12
U. of California, Berkeley	108,828,000	16	175,273,000	13
U. of California, San Francisco	117,302,000	12	169,436,000	14
Harvard U.	119,955,000	11	169,074,000	15
U. of Texas, Austin	88,395,000	20	168,931,000	16
Pennsylvania State U.	94,326,000	19	165,841,000	17
U. of Pennsylvania	111,185,000	14	158,334,000	18
Columbia U.	133,018,000	9	149,904,000	19
Yale U.	116,943,000	13	145,818,000	20
U. of California, Davis	56,622,000	36	143,798,000	21
U. of Arizona	65,024,000	30	138,726,000	22
U. of Southern California	101,749,000	18	134,995,000	23
U. of Maryland, College Park	55,194,000	38	126,239,000	24
U. of Georgia	35,261,000	65	124,442,000	25
Ohio State U.	58,555,000	34	123,246,000	26
Georgia Inst. of Technology	63,132,000	31	120,342,000	27
U. of Colorado	83,144,000	21	112,276,000	28
Michigan State U.	44,989,000	50	111,810,000	29
Purdue U.	56,302,000	37	107,131,000	30
U. of Florida	49,311,000	46	104,245,000	31
Washington U.	77,757,000	23	103,419,000	32
North Carolina State U.	33,662,000	68	102,647,000	33
Louisiana State U.	31,089,000	75	102,070,000	34
U. of Rochester †	80,322,000	22	101,598,000	35
New York U.	76,126,000	24	98,924,000	36
Rutgers U.	27,178,000	79	94,555,000	37
U. of North Carolina, Chapel Hill ...	72,529,000	27	93,754,000	38
U. of Chicago †	75,889,000	25	91,879,000	39
Baylor College of Medicine	49,834,000	44	90,179,000	40
Duke U.	67,925,000	29	89,556,000	41
Northwestern U.	49,286,000	47	88,920,000	42
California Inst. of Technology†	71,086,000	28	86,565,000	43
U. of Pittsburgh	62,060,000	32	84,183,000	44
Carnegie Mellon U.	53,817,000	41	83,763,000	45

	U.S funds for research & development		Total funds for research & development	
	Amount	Rank	Amount	Rank
U. of Connecticut	$36,884,000	63	$81,575,000	46
Virginia Polytechnic Inst. & State U.	32,129,000	70	80,552,000	47
U. of Massachusetts	44,256,000	51	79,814,000	48
Oregon State U...................	46,774,000	48	79,715,000	49
U. of Iowa	57,159,000	35	79,090,000	50
Iowa State U. †	19,682,000	97	78,351,000	51
Yeshiva U.	59,768,000	33	73,773,000	52
U. of Alabama, Birmingham	54,534,000	39	72,692,000	53
Case Western Reserve U.	53,580,000	42	70,850,000	54
State U. of New York, Buffalo	51,212,000	43	70,474,000	55
U. of Utah	54,226,000	40	68,194,000	56
Rockefeller U.	37,983,000	60	66,760,000	57
U. of Texas System Cancer Center ...	22,162,000	89	65,417,000	58
Indiana U.	44,211,000	52	65,341,000	59
U. of Miami	38,052,000	59	65,158,000	60
Princeton U.	43,505,000	53	65,089,000	61
U. of Illinois, Chicago	34,570,000	66	64,701,000	62
U. of Virginia	41,267,000	55	63,861,000	63
U. of Texas Health Science Center, Dallas	45,382,000	49	62,907,000	64
U. of Missouri, Columbia	20,250,000	95	61,212,000	65
U. of Tennessee, Knoxville	28,752,000	78	60,096,000	66
Emory U.	36,698,000	64	58,889,000	67
New Mexico State U.	37,904,000	61	58,672,000	68
Boston U.......................	49,406,000	45	58,299,000	69
U. of Hawaii, Manoa	34,472,000	67	57,345,000	70
U. of Nebraska, Lincoln	24,512,000	84	56,066,000	71
U. of Kentucky	26,261,000	80	55,042,000	72
State U. of New York, Stony Brook ..	39,445,000	56	54,219,000	73
U. of Cincinnati	32,044,000	71	53,804,000	74
Colorado State U.	38,961,000	57	52,619,000	75
U. of California, Irvine	38,138,000	58	51,691,000	76
U. of California, Riverside	15,001,000	108	51,158,000	77
U. of Kansas	22,941,000	86	50,603,000	78
Washington State U...............	21,274,000	94	48,865,000	79
Woods Hole Oceanographic Institute	42,239,000	54	48,061,000	80
Auburn U.	13,446,000	117	48,045,000	81
Oklahoma State U.	9,575,000	138	47,420,000	82
Tufts U.	37,148,000	62	46,497,000	83
Clemson U.	9,016,000	139	46,495,000	84
Florida State U.	21,416,000	93	46,420,000	85
City U. of New York, Mount Sinai School of Medicine	31,024,000	76	46,137,000	86
U. of Maryland, Baltimore	26,244,000	81	45,523,000	87
U. of Oklahoma	14,453,000	111	45,350,000	88
U. of New Mexico	29,096,000	77	45,333,000	89

	U.S funds for research & development		Total funds for research & development	
	Amount	Rank	Amount	Rank
Vanderbilt U.	31,343,000	74	43,589,000	90
U. of California, Santa Barbara	32,856,000	69	42,704,000	91
Utah State U.	22,109,000	90	41,343,000	92
Virginia Commonwealth U.	31,612,000	73	41,016,000	93
Kansas State U.	13,270,000	118	40,587,000	94
Mississippi State U.	12,387,000	125	40,405,000	95
Wayne State U.	16,927,000	103	39,335,000	96
Arizona State U.	14,009,000	114	38,763,000	97
Tulane U.	21,836,000	92	38,393,000	98
Brown U.	32,024,000	72	38,110,000	99
Georgetown U.	24,477,000	85	35,981,000	100
Total, 100 institutions ...	$6,184,538,000		$9,980,550,000	
Total, all institutions	$7,325,710,000		$12,081,531,000	

Note: Figures cover only research-and-development expenditures in science and engineering, and exclude spending in such disciplines as the arts, education, the humanities, law and physical education.
Because some institutions have developed new methods to report their research expenditures more accurately, comparisons with earlier years may not be appropriate.

* Includes the Applied Physics Laboratory with $342-million in total and $338-million in federally funded research-and-development expenditures.
† Excludes research expenditures at university-associated federally funded research-and-development centers.

Journalism, where the author of this book teaches, underwent a rigorous evaluation by an agency known as the Accrediting Council on Education in Journalism and Mass Communications before receiving a clean bill of health in the form of accreditation—at this writing only one of two such accredited programs in Indiana. This is not to say that a student-athlete cannot receive a fine education in a non-accredited program, but if it isn't accredited, he or she should at the very least ask questions to try to determine beforehand if that program has any serious deficiencies.

Students should remember that they are going to college to help improve themselves as thinkers and leaders.

The first place they need to show leadership is in their choice of school. According to the education editor of the *New York Times,* Edward B. Fiske, "College admissions is now becoming a buyer's market." The declining birthrate, says Fiske, means that "colleges are finding it increasingly difficult to fill their classes or, in the case of highly selective ones, to maintain the academic quality of their freshman class."[14] Hence, a highly capable student who is also a blue-chip athlete is now in the best possible bargaining position to gain admission to a truly fine program. If scholar-athletes settle for a second-class education because they are uninformed or too lazy to do any legwork on their own, they are cheating themselves of an opportunity that won't come around twice during their lifetimes. One way they can become more informed is to carefully read some of the books that rate various institutions, including the *Selected Guide to Colleges* (4th ed., 1988).[15]

Students and parents must learn to distinguish recruiting hype from reality, and they must not become victims of vanity or even their dreams. To be sure, many fine universities in this country do also have fine athletic programs. Michigan, Notre Dame, and the University of California at Los Angeles (UCLA) fall into this category. Then again, these institutions are so selective as to be all but out of the question except for truly superior student-athletes. A university such as Northwestern—to name one Big Ten school—has a so-so athletic program but truly fine academic offerings that merit consideration by both students and parents. In addition, schools such as Northwestern never risk NCAA scrutiny for recruiting violations because they keep their athletic programs beyond reproach.

"When a school comes under investigation from a newspaper or the NCAA, the first thing you hear that school say is that 'this is going on everywhere—why are they picking on us?' " said *Lexington Herald-Leader* reporter Jeffrey Marx, winner of a Pulitzer Prize for his investigation of irregularities in the University of Kentucky basketball program. "[But] I'm not sure it's going on everywhere. I went to Northwestern where I don't think it was going on. In fact, we wrote a little story about Northwestern . . . when they turned themselves into the Big Ten Conference, because they had improperly given away a box of M & M's to a recruit during a basketball game. So I don't think this thing [cheating] is going on everywhere, but there probably aren't many schools that could stand up to close scrutiny over a long period of time."[16]

In other words, the responsibility is squarely upon the student-athlete to select the right school, not because of its winning record, but because it plays with integrity. The minute coaches learn that they no longer can buy players with impunity, they'll change their methods. If blue-chip athletes have the courage to say that they won't attend Institution X or Institution Y because those schools are on NCAA probation or because they offered improper recruiting inducements, the bad press attending that kind of announcement can have far-reaching effects on college athletics. If athletes are offered improper inducements and they stay silent, the improprieties are certain to continue.

However, just because an institution has been penalized in the past by the NCAA may not be sufficient reason for a recruit to write that school off. In fact, in some instances, tough NCAA scrutiny may cause a former outlaw institution to toe the line even more than schools that have never been investigated. Southern Methodist University, for example, suffered the "death penalty" for infractions and was not able to resume playing football until 1989. To make sure no new violations occurred, SMU decided to spend $50,000 a year on preventive measures. Mustang recruits now must pass background checks, and the expenses of football players are audited.[17]

Another school that's taken its share of bad press for athletic scandals is Memphis State University, but administrators there tried for a while to bury their deserved bad image. "It didn't take a Rhodes scholar to look at [our] graduation rates and to see we weren't getting the job done," Charles Cavagnaro, the MSU athletics director admitted to *The Chronicle of Higher Education.*[18]

There is no question that MSU has traditionally exploited athletes, minorities in particular. The Memphis chapter of the National Association for the Advancement of Colored People (NAACP) in May 1985 blasted then–Memphis State basketball coach Dana Kirk, noting that only twenty-two of his players—including only six black athletes—had graduated from the program since 1970. These rates were among the lowest in the nation. Another scandal, reported by *The Sporting News,* had a University of Maryland football player being lured to Memphis State with promises of a car and cash.

In the last three years, Memphis State has implemented many positive changes, including emphasizing classroom achievement. By 1988, the school elevated its graduation rate by 50 percent. To keep athletes honest, MSU requires them to punch a time clock when they enter and leave a study hall, and their privileges increase as their gradepoint averages increase.

"The goal is this," MSU academic director Timothy L. Sumner told *The Chronicle of Higher Education.* "If one of our kids fails, it can only be for two reasons—he's not capable of doing it, or he didn't want to. The old cop-outs are gone: The coach didn't push him, he didn't get enough academic support, he didn't have enough time. We're doing everything we can for him. But finally, the burden is on the kid, and that's the way it should be."[19]

ACADEMIC
RESPONSIBILITY

One reason colleges are hustling to improve their academic image is that they fear court action. In a 1982 landmark court case that revealed how athletes have been given preferential treatment to keep them eligible, Dr. Jan Kemp, a University of Georgia English professor, sued the school after she was fired for refusing to raise the failing grades of athletes. A jury awarded her more than $2.5 million in back pay and damages.

Kemp had also objected when nine football players were transferred from remedial to regular classes in 1981, simply to ensure their eligibility for a bowl game. Testimony showed that an athlete who attended as few as two sociology lectures received a grade of C instead of an F.

There is considerable evidence that athletes were kept eligible—and that some even received undergraduate degrees—because coaches and athletic directors played fast and loose with transcripts. In his book, *Out of Their League,* former pro football player Dave Meggyesy alleged that while he played college ball at Syracuse there were players who received summer-school credit for courses they never took. Meggyesy felt that coaches had done their players no favor by committing academic fraud.

"After years of this special treatment, ballplayers begin to lose sight of the fact that this immunity is only temporary," wrote Meggyesy. "There are few more pathetic sights than a former college football hero walking around campus unnoticed. The same university that used to fix his grades . . . and give him money under the table has now turned its back on him. You see a lot of guys whose life actually stopped after their last college game." [1]

Today, athletic directors either fire or reassign coaches caught in such chicanery. California recruiting director Sam Parker and kicker Steve Loop were severely dealt with when an investigation showed that Loop's transcript from a junior college had been doctored. Cal athletic director Dave Maggard reassigned Parker and ruled Loop ineligible. [2]

A major responsibility that athletes must take for themselves—particularly athletes who attend inner-city high schools—is to make certain that an opportunity for a college degree is not delayed or lost because of a failure to score sufficiently high on the Scholastic Aptitude Test (SAT) or American College Testing Assessment. The NCAA's Proposition 48 and Proposal 42 have set minimum academic standards for incoming freshmen athletes.

These controversial proposals have drawn praise from some educators and condemnation from others. Proposition 48 mandates that incoming freshmen student-athletes have a grade-point average of 2.0 in an approved core curriculum. That curriculum must include eleven academic courses, of which there must be a minimum of three years in English, two years in mathematics, two years in social science, and two years in natural or physical science (including a laboratory course if offered). Furthermore, it mandates that student-athletes score a minimum of a 700 combined score (verbal and math sections) on the Scholastic Aptitude Test or a 15 composite score on the American College Test. This score must be achieved by July 1 immediately preceding an athlete's enrollment into college in the autumn.

Proposal 42, which will go into effect in 1990 unless it is thrown out by the NCAA's membership before then, sets up even stricter academic standards. This legislation prevents schools from awarding athletic scholarships to students who fail to completely meet the standards of Proposition 48. Simply stated, those who have not fulfilled all of Proposition 48's minimum requirements cannot receive athletic scholarships during their freshmen year. In addition, these students must sit out during the first year of school and are allowed only three years of athletic eligibility.

The single biggest drawback to these proposals is the way they have closed the door to many athletes—most of them black—who attend inner-city schools and have poor scores. A 1987 survey at twenty-three southern schools by the *Atlanta Constitution* found that 50 of 53 players made ineligible by the bylaw were black. Another survey, by the *Dallas Times-Herald,* revealed that 175 of 206 Proposition 48 casualties in 1985 were black players.

As a result, not everyone has applauded the NCAA's diligence in enforcing high academic standards. "I ain't ready to turn this world over to just intelligent people," said comedian Jerry Clower, a onetime Mississippi State football player. "I want some average, slow thinking good ol' boys occasionally to have some input in how this country's run."

Perhaps the best thing about Proposition 48 is that it has made coaches more aware of the importance of academics. In fact, many college coaches now boast as often about their players' scholastic achievements as they do about their athletic prowess. In August 1987, UCLA announced that all of its basketball recruits met Proposition 48 standards.

"Last semester we had six players with 3.0 or better grade averages and a team average of 2.72," Minnesota basketball coach Clem Haskins told *USA Today* reporter Karen Allen in February 1987. "That, I'm proud of."[3]

But other coaches who traditionally support academics are on record as being opposed to this attitude. "We've got more kids now who have lost their aspiration level than at any time in the history of athletics," complained Temple basketball coach John Chaney to *USA Today.* "It'll make football like it was when I played at Georgia," Auburn coach Pat Dye told sports columnist Joe Marcin. "Players will be smaller and slower—they'll be mostly white. I'm not saying black kids [only] will suffer. There'll be white kids who'll suffer, too."[4]

Dye, and Clemson football coach Danny Ford, insist that students who stay in school four years are better off than they would have been even if they don't graduate. "It's not important that a person gets a degree," concluded Dye. "What's important is that he gets something beneficial from the college experience."[5]

Not quite as opinionated as Pat Dye is University of Maryland chancellor John Slaughter, but his actions demonstrate his reluctance to strengthen his university's academic reputation at the expense of its sports teams. Slaughter refused to accept a recommendation of a taskforce committee formed at his school in the wake of basketball All-American Len Bias's tragic cocaine-induced death, in spite of the fact that studies showed Terrapin athletes had a ghastly graduation rate. The task force had recommended admitting to the school only those students who had achieved at least average scores on standardized tests. Although *The Sporting News* blasted Slaughter, calling his decision "hypocritical," the chancellor defended himself, saying that ruling freshman with poor scores ineligible would "make it very difficult for some of our intercollegiate programs to have successful teams."[6]

Author John F. Rooney, Jr., himself a college professor, finds it "appalling" that so many coaches defend poor graduation rates and the acceptance of subpar students into programs and, in defending their positions, maintain that even athletes who fail their classes benefit from the college experience. "Growth and education by contagion is now being falsely promoted as an alternative to the real thing," says Rooney. "Being exposed to education is . . . not the same as being educated."[7]

Most athletic conferences and coaches have jumped on the academic bandwagon—if only to protect their institutions' reputations. The Southeastern Conference in 1988 phased out the awarding of athletic scholarships to nonqualifying freshmen, and there were predictions that the Pacific-10 and Big Eight would soon follow suit. Coach Jerry Tarkanian, as late as February 1987, had graduated only twenty-three of his sixty-seven players—according to *USA Today*—mainly because of Nevada–Las Vegas's policy of signing junior college players with questionable academic records. But even UNLV has seen the light. Tarkanian told *USA Today* writer David Leon Moore that he has gone all-out to graduate players. "We probably do more now for our players academically than anybody in the country," said Tarkanian. "We have two full-time advisers, plus a part-time adviser."[8]

But Tarkanian also represents a growing trend among many of today's coaches who believe that players must take more responsibility for their actions. After all, most nonathletes who graduate make it through their college years without a tenth of the advisory or tutorial support available to athletes. Those athletes who have the ability to do well in their classes but fail to do so because of laziness or poor application to their studies must shoulder some of the blame.

"You're not gonna graduate everybody," said UNLV's Tarkanian. "What we give them is an opportunity. Then it's their job to get an education. Sometimes I get offended at everything you gotta do. It kinda bothers me that you gotta wake 'em up and get 'em to class."[9]

Oklahoma's outspoken Billy Tubbs agrees with that assessment, complaining that the NCAA's regulations are causing him to act anything like a basketball coach. "What coaching's coming down to is being a warden," complained Tubbs.[10]

The evidence is clear, however, that despite some unhappiness with Proposition 48, the measure is here to stay. Athletes can and must take their studies seriously if they are to play ball. Coaches already are passing over those who do very poorly on the SAT test in favor of lesser athletes with a better chance of playing all four years. Cheating is no solution either. When an athlete does badly on one SAT test and then his or her SAT score jumps considerably, the case is turned over to the American Arbitration Association. In fact, even if an athlete hasn't cheated, there is a penalty involved. Players at Pittsburgh and Kentucky recently sat out one entire season while the arbitrators examined the test results. Whether this is fair or not isn't the issue here. Athletes must be aware of this policy and strive to get a good score the first time they take the SAT or ACT.

How can student-athletes score higher on these examinations? Clearly, preparation for these tests is essential. Waiting until one's senior year to get cracking is too late. Those who score highest on the SAT and ACT have been those who have taken education seriously all their lives.

But it's never too late to begin to cultivate good habits.

It's been observed by many experts that standardized tests separate readers from nonreaders. Those students with a limited vocabulary and poor reading comprehension are at a particular disadvantage. Hence, it's a good idea to acquire a lifelong reading habit. Start slowly—perhaps twenty to thirty minutes a day—with materials you really want to read—copies of *Sport* or *Sports Illustrated,* perhaps; then graduate to reading both fiction and nonfiction books.

Students should also take the PSAT—the SAT preliminary test—sometime during the sophomore year to get an accurate assessment of where their strengths and weaknesses lie. It is at this point that a student should seek assistance from a guidance counselor to get help in the form of tutoring or remedial courses. Another good idea is to purchase any one of several excellent books that aim at helping students improve their SAT scores. These books emphasize drillwork and critical thinking skills and are easily obtained at any large bookstore.

Above all, there is no substitute for performing good work in the classroom. Athletes, particularly in inner-city schools with poor academic reputations, must realize that they, in effect, must become their own role models. They must realize that they are competing for admission to colleges not only with their fellow students, but with students across the nation. Getting by used to be good enough for excellent ballplayers to be admitted to college. Today, it means sitting out one's freshman year or, worse, losing an opportunity to go to college.

Student-athletes should take the SAT or ACT test at the first available date in their junior year. They should also know whether the schools of their choice prefer them to take both tests or just one of the two. By taking the test early, those who do poorly can sign up for a second test. But be aware that few scores change significantly upon retaking. Ask your guidance counselor for assistance with forms and understanding deadlines.

Student-athletes are well advised to look at the tests as a challenge rather than an obstacle. Those who cannot meet challenges do not belong in the high-pressure world of college sports. Those who can be successful on the SAT and ACT tests will possess the right mental outlook to meet their biggest challenge of all—maintaining eligibility throughout their college career and leaving the institution with an education and a degree.

DEALING WITH HIGH-PRESSURE TACTICS

It's been said without exaggeration that a coach's alphabet begins with W and ends with L.[1] Winning may not be the only thing to today's college coaches, but many risk losing their jobs by finishing dead last or even as low as second place. Ironically, those coaches with the best tactical skills on the field don't always win. According to writers Kenneth Denlinger and Leonard Shapiro, "It is an athletic maxim that a [coach] with no special skills can win games if he recruits well, and that a tactician without talented players is a [coach] soon without a job."[2]

In short, coaches either learn to play the recruiting game and play it well, or they must find some less demanding field to enter. "If you can't recruit, you aren't going to make it," said UCLA basketball coach Jim Harrick.[3] And as University of Missouri–Kansas City basketball coach Lee Hunt told the Associated Press, "Recruiting is like shaving—miss a day, and you look like a bum."[4]

A *Rocky Mountain News* survey of major college football coaches reported that nine in ten felt "intense pressure to win—and win often."[5] Florida State head coach Bobby

Bowden told the newspaper that some coaches reacted to the stress by cheating. "The win-at-all-costs attitude forces coaches to take shortcuts to succeed," said Bowden. "The shortcut is to buy players."

Basketball coaches were not included in the survey, but, not surprisingly, big-time coaches in that sport also say they feel pressured to win. Those that fail to guide their teams to postseason tournaments usually worry whether their contracts will be renewed. "It is the law of jungle survival," said Dean Smith, head coach at the University of North Carolina, commenting on the approximately sixty Division I coaching changes that occur each season. "I don't like it and wish I could do something about it. But that's the way it is."[6]

At many schools the pressure is especially intense when one sport generates the lion's share of the athletic department's income. The University of Kentucky's basketball program is a case in point, since for many years it carried a traditionally weak football program. This is also true of the football program at the University of Washington, which generates 85 percent of the athletic budget.

Unfortunately, head coaches pass their own fears of failure and the unreasonable expectations of alumni onto their recruiters. The recruiters, in turn, feel they've failed at their job unless they consistently land the nation's blue-chip players. As a result, the recruiting process becomes one of the most pressure-filled situations of a young man or woman's lifetime. Imagine the pressure put upon Oklahoma recruit Elvis Peacock who received ten visits from that school's head coach and his assistants. The Sooners spent $10,000 in travel and expenses to get Peacock's signature on a letter of intent. Of course, Oklahoma wasn't the only school pursuing Peacock, and his parents wound up changing their phone number "three or four times."[7] A San Antonio high school football player named Warren

McVea turned down fifty colleges before choosing the University of Houston.[8]

Coaches do whatever it takes to land top athletes—including buying them. "The idea is to sprinkle a little money here and a little there and, pretty soon, you've bought yourself a player," wrote *USA Today* in an editorial condemning this practice in college athletics. Coaches and their recruiters—as well as boosters—don't always feel bound by the social rules and regulations that the rest of society feels duty-bound to obey. What they may view as being conscientious and persistent often amounts to outright invasion of the privacy of high school athletes and their families.

Rather than tout the educational value of the institution they represent, recruiters too often underestimate the character and intelligence of young people today, asking vapid questions about the athlete's preference for members of the opposite sex. The student-athlete, unaware of NCAA procedures (or, if aware, too awed to object), often accepts improper transportation to a college's sporting event or takes trinkets or T-shirts with the school's name printed on them.

Or, all too often, a greedy or misinformed parent or guardian falls into a recruiter's trap and accepts improper gifts or favors. More than one parent who is out of work or stuck in a dead-end job (or who wants to move close to campus to live near the student-athlete) has found an offer of steady employment too tempting to refuse. Moreover, college coaches and administrators justify offering these improper jobs by calling themselves do-gooders when the NCAA catches them. Such was the case at Clemson University when coaches helped the mother of a quarterback find work. "We have discarded principles," former University of Michigan athletic director Fritz Crisler lamented to *Sports Illustrated.* "We are nourishing a monster."[9]

Also, too often, the people in the athletic department that the student-athlete turns to for advice—the coaches, respected alumni, even the academic counselors—offer advice that is not in the young person's best interest. Witness all the transcripts that have been altered, the easy courses athletes have been "encouraged" to take, and the all-but-worthless degrees that have been granted by so-called responsible institutions of higher learning.

"Colleges teach values to students by the standards they set for themselves," said the Carnegie Foundation for the Advancement of Teaching in 1987, which advocates revoking accreditation when recruiting violations are discovered. "But we believe real reform will come only when a wave of moral indignation sweeps the campuses. Perhaps the time has come for faculty and students at universities engaged in big-time athletics to organize a day of protest, setting aside a time to examine how the purposes of the university are being subverted and how integrity is lost." Concluded the Carnegie Foundation's Ernest L. Boyer, "Big-time sports are out of control."[10]

Sports Illustrated once reported on the crisis facing college football, concluding that the recruitment of high school players and their subsidization "have in recent years gone far beyond the limits of the tolerable." Some athletes fail to make passing grades their senior year simply because they cannot handle the hounding of recruiters and manage their studies at the same time.

In addition to frequent phoning, some coaches write notes on a weekly or monthly basis. Others telegram athletes to show their interest. Many others demand game films of the prospect or ask that long questionnaires be answered. Some appeal to the macho instincts of a player. "The challenge is there," one Texas coach used to tell potential recruits. "The question is whether you're man enough to meet it."[11]

Recruiting has become a science. Computer files or manila file folders are kept on college-bound high school players, particularly on those in the immediate area. Coaches often get information on potential stars from alumni clubs and paid scouts across the country; high-priced reports are also sold to them by various independent scouting services. Athletic departments subscribe to many newspapers, and these are culled by graduate assistants and other athletic-department employees to keep tabs on talented athletes.

Coaches fight for every recruiting advantage. Another thing the blue-chip athlete must get straight is whether or not it matters that a given team has won a national championship or showcased a player who has won a major award such as the Heisman Trophy or Butkus Award. Bobby Bowden, for example, says that he regards all awards "as recruiting tools."[12]

On the plus side for the athlete, the attention of the media certainly is on a school that boasts championships and major awards. This is especially valuable for those blue-chip players with enough ability themselves to vie for the same honors, or for those who love playing for a winner: "If possibly being a part of a national championship team" is important to you, says Kentucky assistant coach James Dickey, "riding the bench may be better than playing full-time at some lesser institution."[13]

On the minus side, players who fall a bit short of superstar status may not be wise to sign with such schools. If riding the bench (and possibly not having your scholarship renewed) is not your cup of tea, you may wish to look at less publicized programs.

Athletes should be aware that college coaches would be foolish not to trust the ratings of certain tried-and-true high school coaches who consistently turn out fine athletes. Gridiron coach Rollie Robbins, in fifteen years at

Interlake High School in Bellevue, Washington, has graduated more than fifty players who earned college scholarships, including six who went on to play professional football.[14]

But occasionally, high school coaches, by guaranteeing that they can deliver such blue-chippers, will consciously or unconsciously use the so-called tenderloin athlete to get them into top assistant positions. The practice is common, but there is little the NCAA can do about it. By way of example, the NCAA allowed Lower Richland (South Carolina) High School basketball coach Jim Childers to continue recruiting his own star, 6-11, 265-pound Stanley Roberts, even though Childers had already accepted an assistant-coach position at LSU. Childers was the fifth high school coach to sign with the LSU Tigers as an assistant since 1979; all five brought their star performers with them to join Coach Dale Brown's staff. The other four were recruit Rudy Macklin and Coach Ron Abernathy, recruit Howard Carter and his coach, Rick Huckabay, recruit Tom Curry and his coach, Gary Duhe, and recruit Nikita Wilson and his coach, Mike Mallet.

Players who find themselves in this position must sort out the situation for themselves. They should remember that their first responsibility is to advance their own careers, not those of their high school coaches.

If a high school coach accepts an assistant job at LSU or Oklahoma or anywhere else, the player should immediately check out the academic program at that college. Once again, the first choice should be to go to a school that can train athletes for the job or profession of their choice. If the school is unsuitable, a player must have the courage to tell that high school coach to stop recruiting him or her. If the coach persists despite a player's protests, the NCAA should be contacted.

On the other hand, if the school's academic program

suits a player, and the opportunity to play college ball in the company of a favorite high school coach is appealing, the player may be wise to sign with that program. However, to avoid later regrets and hard feelings, the athlete should visit at least two or three other college campuses. The right choice may be difficult to make under the pressures that a high-school-coach-turned-college-assistant can put on a player, but it's not impossible.

To be sure, many high school coaches are unselfish individuals. There have been high school coaches who have demonstrated that they have the best interests of their athletes—not themselves—at heart by turning in colleges who participate in recruiting shenanigans. For example, the former high school coach Ronald McClain called the NCAA in 1986 to report that his school, Memphis State, had contacted the basketball star at a time of the year when contacts are not permitted. [15]

Dan Jenkins once wrote a description of the recruiting game for *Sports Illustrated* that sums up the feeding frenzy that coaches indulge in when they are in the pursuit of a blue-chip athlete. As the writer points out, coaches leave no cliché unturned as they pursue the one that they hope won't get away.

"Every year he turns up in some little dry-bed town, where the folks are God-fearing, mother-loving, flag-saluting and psychoneurotic about football," wrote Jenkins. "He is big, tough, intelligent, unselfish, a leader. And fast? He runs the quarter in 46 flat—in the rain. And his arm? Why, it's like one of those bazookies that we kill the Red Commonist (sic) Nazi menace with. Everybody in town has seen him flick the ball 60 yards on his knees with two linebackers jerking on his face guard. . . . He's got it all, which is why [Notre Dame] and [Alabama] and [Texas] and the Detroit Tigers and the Boston Celtics and the Morgan Guaranty Trust have all been trying to sign him up since he was in the fourth grade. And it is why whoever winds up with him will announce it in a press conference on the battleship *Missouri*, and why those who don't will go running off to the NCAA and the FBI."[16]

What makes a blue-chip athlete? An outstanding and consistent record of game performances against stellar competition as a high school player, certainly, but also blazing speed, sufficient weight and height for the athlete's position, as well as (in recent years) enough intelligence to pass college entrance examinations. Former Michigan State football coach Duffy Daugherty once stated his needs poetically: "We like them big at Michigan State, but we'll settle for players with three kinds of bones—a funny bone, a wishbone and a backbone. The funny bone is to enjoy a laugh, even at one's own expense. The wishbone is to think big, set one's goals high and to have dreams and ambitions. The backbone . . . is what a boy needs to . . . go to work and make all those dreams come true."[17]

Florida State football coach Bobby Bowden looks for mental and physical toughness in a recruit, saying flat-out that many of today's athletes lack such a quality. "There is a change [in athletes today], but it's a change that relates to a change in society," maintains Bowden. "We've gotten lax in our society, and our kids have gotten lax. Physically, they're bigger, stronger, faster. But I don't know if they're as tough."

Bowden also says that today's athletes tend to challenge authority more readily, but he doesn't necessarily feel this is a bad change. "I didn't use to waste time to say 'Why,' " says Bowden. "I said, 'This is what we're going to do, now get it done.' Nowadays, they need an explanation. Yessirree, I think they've got to have it. If you don't give it to them, you might have a hard time. But if you *can* tell them why, you're likely to get what you want."

Unfortunately, things are getting more difficult for non–blue-chippers to attract scholarships, particularly in football. A rule instituted by the 1987 President's Commission of the NCAA has made it difficult for marginal football players—not blue-chippers—to attract college offers. The rule states that football games could be evaluated after November 1 only. In many states, such as Indiana, the regular football season is over and playoff games are under way before recruiters can legally come out to watch high schools play. In Indiana, after November 1, only 40 out of 312 schools in the state had the opportunity to have a personal visit from a recruiter. "To be quite honest about it, I and a lot of other high school coaches aren't too happy about it," Dick Dullaghan, football coach at Ben Davis High School, told the *Indianapolis Star.* "There are many kids who are marginal out there who are not getting looked at. . . . It's not the top-of-the-line kid who's getting hurt by this, but the kids at the next level and the next level."

Those athletes who do get recruited will receive a letter of agreement saying that the recruited athlete promises to play for the undersigned institution. These letters of intent are not binding unless signed by the athlete and the athlete's parents if he or she is under eighteen years old. Athletes should never announce the decision to attend a particular institution unless they have their parents' signed permission. To make an announcement and then retract it is always embarrassing. Letters expire fourteen days from the day the athletic director signs the letter if the player fails to also sign it. Athletes must remember that this letter is not the same as a statement from the university that financial aid has been awarded, and that they should never sign up until that statement has also been sent by the university. Once athletes sign an official letter of intent, all other institutions (who subscribe to the National Letter of

Intent program) are obligated to stop their recruiting efforts toward the signees.

Letters of intent usually are binding on the player, but there are exceptions. In March 1987, the National Letter of Intent Steering Committee overturned a document that Los Angeles prep star Sean Higgins, a 6-8 forward whom many sportswriters favorably compared with Danny Manning, had signed with UCLA although he had made an oral commitment to Michigan. But after Higgins complained that his parents had forced him to sign with the Bruins against his will, the signed letter was ruled invalid despite denials of improper conduct given by Higgins's mother and stepfather. Consequently, Higgins signed another letter of intent with the University of Michigan, his original choice.[18]

Letters of intent may also be broken if a college violated NCAA regulations during the recruiting process. Such was the case with a Douglas, Georgia, high school football player named George Smith, who accused the Georgia Bulldogs of recruiting improprieties and was allowed to sign with Texas A & M.

The penalty is severe for athletes who sign a letter of intent and break the contract without official permission. They must wait one year before receiving financial aid based upon athletic ability from another institution.

Ignorance of the rules concerning letters of intent or eligibility is no excuse. It is the responsibility of the recruit, the recruiter, and the high school coach to know the NCAA bylaws regarding contact and evaluation. Information prospective student-athletes receive from other sources is not always accurate and, thus, could adversely affect their college eligibility status. The NCAA's assistant executive director, William B. Hunt, can answer questions posed by institutions.

It is important for athletes to recognize that recruiters

do not have carte blanche to pursue them at all times. The NCAA has stipulated several times a year as so-called dead periods when recruiters cannot actively visit high school players on or off campus. In 1988, for example, men's basketball dead periods included March 31 to April 5, to coincide with the NCAA Final Four, and from April 11 to April 13, to coincide with National Letter of Intent signings. In addition, the NCAA also mandates several "quiet periods" when no *off*-campus contact or evaluation is permitted; there were four such quiet periods in 1988. The women's basketball programs also had dead and quiet periods, which only occasionally coincided with the men's programs.

In addition, the NCAA has limited its Division I school representatives to observing only a certain percentage of a player's games. For example, recruiters can attend no more than four men's basketball games (three for women) in one academic year, including regular high school games, recreational league games, and all-star games. However, practice sessions and so-called one-on-one competitions do not count as game observations and are currently unrestricted.

If coaches do not observe the NCAA rules in recruiting, an athlete can and should object. Coaches love to defeat one another in recruiting wars almost as much as they do in games; and some coaches, unfortunately, who would never cheat to win on the court or playing field, see nothing wrong with bending recruiting rules.

In 1987, *The Sporting News* reported how the University of Florida practically stole away a football player committed to archrival Florida State. Just weeks earlier, recruit Terrence Barber told reporters that he was ready to sign with FSU's Bobby Bowden. "Florida State stresses academics more than either Miami or Florida," said Barber. "I know at that school the degree I want [in marketing] is there for me. Miami and Florida were just stressing football." But the Florida coaching staff persuaded another new recruit, a Heisman Trophy–quality running back named Emmitt Smith, to talk with Barber. Smith ought to get into sales after his football career ends, because in just one phone call, he persuaded Barber to come to Florida. And once the Gators had Barber committed, their recruiting staff tried some cloak-and-dagger stuff to keep him under lock and key. "Our coaches . . . couldn't find him," Wayne Hogan, a spokesman for Florida State, told reporters.[19]

Some recruiters love the gamesmanship associated with recruiting, but unless players think of themselves as no more than pawns on a chessboard, they should not allow themselves to be manipulated. If Barber was really sold on Florida after talking to Smith, why didn't he just call Bowden or his coaches with his decision? He also should never have given a verbal commitment to FSU in the first place. He came across to the public as someone who did not know his own mind. What kind of opinion can a coach have of someone like this? One supposed reason athletes play sports is to gain maturity. Learning to play the recruiting game properly is an important first step for every player.

5

WHEN THE RECRUITER COMES CALLING

Home visits are particularly popular with recruiters because they can size up the lifestyle and economic needs of a prospective athlete at a glance. Recruiters can determine if the athlete or a parent may be vulnerable because of pressing economic need. Coaches can often judge a player's potential success by the quality of his or her home life. [1]

No knight ever courted fair maiden as hard as today's recruiters court blue-chip athletes. If staying for dinner with a player's parents will help a recruiting assistant coach close a deal, then he or she will do it with gusto. The best recruiters can chat about the price of fertilizer with rural parents, talk politics with those so inclined, and even sing gospel music if invited into a Southern Baptist parlor.

There's a famous *Time* magazine story about former University of Nebraska head coach (now the athletic director) Bob Devaney, who prided himself on his ability to act the chameleon around the parents of athletes he just had to have. Supposedly, he was so proud of the way he signed West Virginia all-star end Tony Jeter by joining his family's hymnfest, that he tried the same tactic at another prospect's home. Devaney sang himself hoarse with the prospect's mother, but at last even the relentless old coach admitted defeat. The recruit enrolled at the University of Michigan, but Devaney had one small consolation—the prospect's mother enrolled at Nebraska.

In the face of such perseverance, blue-chip athletes and their families need to draw up a set of guidelines before inviting recruiters into their homes. A basic rule of thumb for players is this: Don't let any recruiter into your living room whose school you absolutely can't envision signing with.

USA Today hit the problem squarely on the head in an enlightened editorial headlined "Treat young players with more respect." According to the editorial writer, "Recruiting can be a callous business, with the air of a meat market. The coaches who are trying to entice these teenagers to sign are adults. A 17-year-old . . . is no match for a ruthless, aggressive recruiter."[2]

That being true, it is very important that blue-chip athletes and their families put considerable thought into how they plan to handle the recruiting experience *before* the first recruiter comes calling. The recruiting process isn't all good or all bad and if managed properly can be a positive experience for both parent and athlete. "There is a lot of pressure in being recruited, but I think most of it is self-pressure," wrote blue-chip high school linebacker Ned Bolcar for a *USA Today* column. "The experience is both depressing and enjoyable."[3]

Chart 2 on pages 97–99 of this book can help athletes decide what is the best program for their needs. And although it is true that players may not be able to answer all the questions raised by that chart before they actually talk with recruiters from specific schools, they can and should eliminate schools that do not meet basic criteria.

For example, student-athletes must decide in what part of the country they plan to attend school. Those players who feel that they must stay near home certainly limit their choices to a few specific schools. Recruiters from colleges outside these players' states (or perhaps adjacent states) can and should be discouraged by letter or phone.

On the other hand, players with no reluctance to leave home have far more options. But athletes who easily get homesick and their families must realize that they themselves must pay all costs of transportation. It is illegal for a school or a booster to pay for a plane ride back home to meet a family emergency, for example. The only exception allowed by the NCAA is that athletes can fly to their bowl games from home at the school's expense.

Parents and athletes can visit the local library to read reference books such as *The Places Rated Almanac* to eliminate schools that fail to meet certain requirements in geography, climate, recreational opportunities, and so forth. For example, students who absolutely cannot abide a cold winter climate should eliminate the University of Minnesota from consideration and pay careful attention to recruiters from the University of Miami, the University of Florida, and San Diego State. Students who wish to have camping and fishing opportunities nearby ought to cross urban campuses off their list and stick to campuses with access to relatively unspoiled country such as Florida State, Boise State, and Penn State. Students who are considering colleges in large cities such as Los Angeles, New York, and Boston should bear in mind that expenses for even minimal costs such as movie tickets and restaurant dates can add up.

Once athletes have compiled a list of locations where they feel they can be at least content for four or five years, they can then study one of several commercial guides to college that list schools by majors offered, athletic opportunities, and so forth. These also discuss the "personality" of the various campuses and whether the school is non-selective, somewhat selective, or very selective. Student-athletes can then begin the laborious process of eliminating some schools and putting others on a priority list. High school students should honestly assess their academic and athletic records to choose those colleges with which they believe they can be most compatible.

Of course, the greater an athlete's fame and ability, the more offers he or she can expect to attract and the more picky he or she can be. Athletes with lesser skills or some notoriety may have to be less selective about location, although they should think twice before attending a school that lacks the academic offerings they require. As in all things, the athlete's first priority should be a good education, and there can be no more discouraging course of action than spending four or five years studying a curriculum that one absolutely dislikes.

The blue-chip athlete, in particular, needs to develop an ability to deal with recruiters. Although coaches often act as though recruiting is the highlight of their coaching lives every time they walk into a recruit's home, the more honest among them admit that it's not always fun. "Recruiting drives me nuts," admitted University of Alabama at Birmingham baseball coach Harry Walker to *The Sporting News* following his retirement. "I haven't enjoyed the recruiting, and I haven't enjoyed the bus rides."[4]

As recruiting becomes even more international in scope, and high school teams play football and basketball in such far-flung locations as Finland, Japan, Australia, Africa, and Brazil, recruiters must sometimes travel long distances to sign players. According to *The Sporting News,* one of the longest trips taken by a recruiter was a nine-hour plane trip that University of Colorado assistant coach Les

Miles took from Boulder to Samoa. Although 6-6, 235-pound linebacker Oakland Salavea was living in the United States, Miles made the trip to Salavea's parents overseas to comply with NCAA rules requiring parental signatures on all letters of intent.

Another record for jet-setting was established by Louisiana State basketball coach Dale Brown when he attempted to strengthen a then-sagging program by visiting basketball center Arvidas Sabonis, a member of the USSR national team, in an unsuccessful effort to recruit the 7-2 giant.

If recruiters were unpleasant folks, ditching them would be easy. But the fact is that these ambitious, usually attractive young men and women who come calling are hired by coaches precisely because they are outgoing, attractive, and blessed with an ability to gab. They are trained not to take no for an answer, but that may be precisely the answer that a blue-chip athlete needs to give them—repeatedly if necessary.

The best way for a prospect to handle recruiters is to be courteous but brief. If fifty colleges phone in a single week, a student can waste a tremendous amount of time with a receiver glued to the outer ear. Likewise, a student can find fifty or sixty letters in the mail, along with a half-dozen videotapes, and go crazy in the process of trying to answer them all. Worse, unless a student discourages un-wanted contacts, all these recruiters can and soon will be ringing the doorbell. And they are far easier to get rid of on the phone than they are in person.

Under no circumstances do parents or athletes need to tolerate recruiters camping out on doorsteps or staying long into the night to deliver a pitch. Neither do they have to provide refreshments unless they desire to, nor tolerate smoking in the house or drop-in recruiters who've failed to make an appointment before coming over. Parents are well within their rights to set up specific times and time limits for visitations. Some parents limit their son or daughter to one recruiting visit a day or so many per month. Others insist that recruiters wait until the athlete has completed all homework for the night. If a recruiter's pitch turns into harassment, parents can either terminate all dealings with that representative's school or call the institution's athletic director to register a complaint.

Other persistent callers are those who run basketball summer camps or scouting services such as High Potential in Shepherdsville, Kentucky. Men such as Bob Gibbons of North Carolina and Dave Benezra of Los Angeles are experts at finding excellent basketball players and matching them with recruiters. To be sure, some high school players may welcome assistance from these experts, but the truly big blue-chippers won't usually need their help to gain coaches' attention.

In addition, recruiters will try to get friends, family, and acquaintances of the player to intercede on behalf of the university, and these calls must be discouraged. Athletes must draw the line and cut off all talk with people who have any connection at all with universities that the player considers undesirable. An answering machine can help screen unwanted calls. In extreme cases, the telephone company can assign an unlisted phone number.

Even with recruiters a player *wants* to meet, it is wise for the athlete to play it polite but reserved. The athlete can ultimately sign with only one institution. All the other recruiters are going to be rejected, and none of them is going to be pleased. By the same token, many an athlete has grown attached to a particular recruiter, only to be brokenhearted after receiving a "Dear John" rejection letter because the coaching staff eventually decided the athlete didn't fit into the college's plans.

Getting too friendly with recruiters is dangerous. It

can blind the athlete to the task at hand—choosing a school for that school's sake, not because a recruiter has a rap down pat. This is especially true when recruiters bring their ultimate weapon—the head coach—to meet a prospect. A player who isn't careful will succumb to flattery and sign when the head coach visits, whether or not that coach's school is the "right" one for that athlete.

Orators such as Bo Schembechler have their pitch down to a science after reciting it so many times over to get recruits to come to their schools. At a Dallas special convention of the NCAA in 1987, Bo Schembechler impressed even his fellow coaches with his passion and conviction. "The greatest experience I ever had at my university was my association on that football team," said Schembechler. "Wherever I have coached, I have carried on that premise. . . . I want that experience to be the greatest experience that they have in college." When Schembechler finished speaking, North Carolina State University basketball coach Jim Valvano shook his head in appreciation of Bo's oratory. "I wanted to play," Valvano told an Associated Press reporter. "I wanted to tackle someone from Columbus [site of Ohio State]."

Recruits need to put limits on how much time they spend with recruiters. Former Georgia head football coach Vince Dooley lost a top LaGrange, Georgia, linebacker who had already committed to the Bulldogs after a Clemson recruiter literally "baby-sat" the player, John Johnson, during the two days prior to National Signing Day.[5] All the attention paid recruits is flattering, of course, but if any recruiter begins to overstay his or her welcome, a high school player should tell the recruiter to leave.

Recruits should also have the good sense (even if recruiters don't) to insist that visiting assistant coaches limit their remarks to positive comments about their own programs. Recruiters who resort to saying negative things about their rivals should not be trusted. The athlete should give the recruiter one warning and then, if negativity persists, decline to talk with the recruiter further.

On many occasions, the athlete manages to remain aloof and it is the parents that fall for a recruiter's hard sell. Parents who are especially vulnerable are those who lap up praise for their son or daughter. "You just don't know what it's like to have someone come into your house and tell you how great your child is," said Mike Currence, a high school coach from Massillon, Ohio. "You'll sit up until three in the morning listening to that."[6]

Without question, parents and athletes alike must say goodbye to anyone dangling improper offers, from cash to free dental work. The top recruits, particularly impoverished inner-city minorities, tend to attract the sharks and charlatans among recruiters. "It's dog eat dog. I had a couple junior college recruiters kidnap a player right after a game," complained Al Prewitt, a high school coach in Lexington, Kentucky. "They took the kid and bought him a steak dinner. We had to suspend the kid."[7]

The recruiters who should be trusted are those who make promises that not only are legal but also easily kept. "The only promise I make to the families is that their sons are going to graduate on time," Notre Dame basketball coach Digger Phelps said. "I've had two players leave school early to play professional ball, but they came back and finished in summer school. . . . It's my feeling that between the parents and myself, we'll realign the thinking of that youngster. You can't survive today without [academic] credentials. They must work hard while they're here.

"The one thing I promise parents when I recruit their sons is that their sons will graduate with a degree that means something. That's what higher education and intercollegiate athletics are supposed to be about. . . . Notre

Dame is a unique educational experience in that sense. I want our athletes to know who they are as persons, to give them the confidence to deal with the ups and downs of everyday life."

Purdue head basketball coach Gene Keady agrees with Phelps. "Besides individual character, academic ability is the first priority we have when we are recruiting student-athletes," Keady told the Associated Press. "Sometimes, the higher standards hurt us; but usually, they help. We have to be pretty selective. . . . Smarter players make for a smarter team. They respond to pressure and criticism better, and they are much more coachable."

The home visit is a good time for parents to pin down the head coach or the recruiter as to the specifics of a scholarship, always keeping in mind that no promise made is binding until something is in writing. Coaches must demonstrate familiarity with the athlete's academic background and offer a realistic picture of how the prospect may perform in class. Bron Bacevich, a Cincinnati high school football coach, warns against empty promises, such as "there will be no grade problem in your academic area" to a student-athlete whose high school record indicates otherwise.[8]

The best recruiters are those who keep pressure on recruits and parents to a minimum. Those recruiters who imply that a scholarship won't be around very long if a recruit fails to immediately sign a letter of intent are likely to be bluffing. If the parent threatens to phone the university president, the recruiter usually finds a way to extend the consideration period.

Recruiters can provide exact information on financial aid, but a good rule of thumb for parents and students is: Be wary when recruiters profess to know everything about every department and major their campuses offer. There are informed sources on campus (see Chapter Seven) that can and should be consulted to get a truer picture of the various institutions' academic pluses and minuses.

Parents also should find out exactly how much of a time commitment a recruit is expected to make during the athletic season. Is the student expected not only to practice and play, but also to speak on occasion to booster groups and other organizations? What is the study-hall situation? How many tutors does the athletic department have, and what are their credentials and precise areas of expertise? What is the name of the school's academic counselor, and when can he or she be reached for a phone conversation with the parents or athlete? Does the athletic department pay all tutoring costs, or must players pay all or some out of pocket?

The family must also inquire into the terms of the scholarship. Are there any requirements attached to the scholarship? For example, must a student work any hours to pay for housing costs?

Finally, athletes and parents must satisfy themselves that there is little danger that a university will go on probation or, worse, be given the death penalty anytime soon. Questions must be asked about the status of other sports in the university, since an NCAA investigation of one discipline is often expanded into other areas. Above all, athletes and their families should never ask a coach or recruiter to break or bend the NCAA's rules for them.

"You don't want to owe anything to anyone," said recruit Ned Bolcar in *USA Today.* "You want to start out saying I owe you nothing but my best."[9]

THE RECRUIT
AND THE
HIGH SCHOOL COACH

When does a student-athlete officially become a recruit in the eyes of the NCAA?

According to the official *NCAA Manual*, the first important criterion is the school's intention. If the school merely asks the athlete or the athlete's coach to fill out a questionnaire, the institution has not yet initiated enough effort for the NCAA to consider it officially in pursuit of an athlete. Nor is it recruiting when a member of the athletic staff or a booster "exhibits normal civility" to a student or to that student's family, or offers one complimentary admission to an athletic contest.

On the other hand, the student becomes a recruit if the university athletic department member or representative pays the athlete's way to campus for a visit and/or phones or visits the athlete or athlete's family to discuss recruitment.

Once the university initiates a contact, the athlete's high school coach often becomes an important player in the recruitment process. A student-athlete who lives far from the university is likely to receive a visit at school or home before the university takes on the expense of paying for an official visit to the campus.

Out of courtesy to the high school coach and teaching staff, athletes sometime during their junior year should sit down with the coach and principal or vice-principal to become knowledgeable about whatever procedures and regulations the high school has established to deal with recruiters and visitors (boosters) representing a university's interests.

It is quite possible that a student's high school has established stricter rules regarding contacts with recruiters and/or visits to games and scrimmages than even the NCAA requires. Therefore, the student, the parent, and the high school coach must discuss all these restrictions so that a loss of eligibility or a suspension from the team doesn't inadvertently result. Above all, the blue-chip athlete should never ask to receive treatment different from that accorded other athletes at the high school. The athlete begins to go a long way toward showing maturity when he or she protects the high school's honor and integrity by obeying its recruiting rules.

The athlete must understand that the coach and principal are duty-bound to make sure that the high school's rules are followed. A common complaint of coaches and school employees alike is that a small minority of hotshot college recruiters and boosters show little respect for them and their rules. Therefore, the athlete should not be embarrassed or angry if the high school coach or principal calls a recruiter to task who has ignored or disobeyed certain regulations.

For example, if a recruiter shows up unannounced in the high school coach's office, the coach has the right to demand that the visitor leave at once. Common courtesy dictates that all recruiters should phone ahead to make an appointment to visit a school. Those who drop in because they were "in the neighborhood" are being inconsiderate. What's more, even if the recruiter has an appointment, all visitors must sign in at the main desk as a security measure, as well as show identification when asked.

Another rule that many high school coaches enforce is that recruiters address their entire team on visits to the high school, not just an individual recruit. Once again, the high school coach is operating on his or her own territory, and both the student-athlete and the recruiter must respect that rule even if they disagree with it.

When it becomes apparent that a high school athlete is talented enough to attract recruiting offers, the player and the coach need to have a talk about the student's hopes and plans. The athlete should respectfully listen to the coach's feelings about various colleges and college coaches, but by no means should the coach's opinion be regarded as law. Too often the coach knows a tremendous amount about sports but very little about the wide range of universities and their curriculums. The athlete must also be extremely wary of what a high school coach recommends if the coach has anything to gain from the student's enrollment at a particular college. As we said earlier, many college coaches hire high school coaches as assistants with the expectation that they'll bring their high school star player along with them. Athletes who feel they are being used as a stepping-stone for a high school coach should contact the NCAA in confidence for help and advice.

Athletes should always be considerate to their high school coaches and clear all requests from recruiters through them. For example, the athlete should never assume that it is all right to invite a recruiter to a game or scrimmage without the approval of the coach. Nor should the athlete presume that the coach is eager to spend time in conference with fifty different college recruiters. Before taking the coach's valuable time away from work and family, the blue-chip recruit should prepare a list of no more than a dozen institutions that interest him or her after carefully reading the academic catalogs of all the various institutions, as well as media guides and recruiting brochures. Sure, it's flattering for the athlete to boast to friends that so many schools are in pursuit, but it's not fair to put a coach through such an ordeal.

The head coach of Cincinnati's Roger Bacon High School, Bron Bacevich, wrote an article for the American Football Coaches Association that detailed many of the complaints that high school coaches have regarding recruiters. "Some of the [colleges] are sending out some real creeps to do their recruiting," wrote one coach. "They are discourteous to the people in the school, and a good many of them completely ignore school rules and regulations pertaining to visitors." Another warned that things had deteriorated with recruiters to a point that "we are seriously considering denying these [representatives] the opportunity to visit our school."[1]

The student-athlete needs to be aware of the possible friction between high school coaches and recruiters. After all, the student very much needs letters of recommendation for college admission, not only from the coach but from the high school principal and/or teachers. The athlete also needs to seek advice from these people and a trustworthy guidance counselor. Too often in high school situations, particularly at inner-city high schools, athletes have followed role models who are arrogant and disrespectful to their coaches and teachers. This has a domino effect, since other students in the school in turn look to athletes as *their* role models. High school athletes should set an example in the classroom as well as in athletics. When athletes begin to excel in the classroom and in life, there no longer will be the problems associated with Proposition 48.

Sometime during the junior year, the athlete needs to

make an appointment with the coach for an honest, no-punches-pulled evaluation of his or her potential for college athletics. Only a few players will hear that the coach thinks they are ready for the bruising competition of the Big Ten or the Southeastern Conference. In football, for example, only 3,000 of the roughly 300,000 high school seniors can receive a Division I scholarship, and the odds are equally tough in golf, basketball, wrestling, baseball, and other varsity sports—for women as well as men. A coach may say that a player's ability or size is inadequate for one of the major conferences such as the Pacific-10 but just right for the Middle Atlantic Conference. Above all, the player should not believe all the press clippings or scouting reports that independent agencies put out. Too many surefire blue-chippers—in the estimation of sportswriters and scouts—later fail to blossom in college, much to the frustration of these athletes. No matter how good a recruit looks on paper, no college coach who is truly honest will ever call a prospect a "can't miss" star until that player actually plays against topnotch competition. By the same token, a *Sports Illustrated* article noted that many players, such as Alabama's All-American linebacker Derrick Thomas, are rated very poorly by scouts because they've not fully matured or were overlooked while in high school.

During that meeting with the coach, athletes must ask for an honest evaluation of their strengths and weaknesses—not only as a player but as a person. If a player is a strong performer in more than one sport, does the coach think the athlete should concentrate on one sport or compete in two or more sports?

During the conversation the athlete should ask whether the coach can provide game films in case recruiters request them. The player must ask the coach, "How much input do you honestly want to have in my decision to attend college?" Some coaches want a lot of involvement.

Others, who feel pressured by their jobs and the expectations of alumni and fans, don't want to be bothered at all. If this is the case, a player must try to find a trusted principal, teacher, or guidance counselor who can provide advice. Above all, the athlete must convince the coach that he or she has the high school team's best interests at heart. A player who appears to be looking for personal glory and statistics at the expense of team wins and team glory, risks losing the coach's support.

Perhaps it may come out in the chat that the coach doubts an athlete's dedication. Perhaps in the past the player has failed to show the maturity in academics and athletics that is needed for success in college. In that case, the athlete must assure the coach that he or she is eager to prove the coach wrong, but once the player makes such an assertion, he or she must be prepared to come through in the classroom and in competition.

Finally, it is extremely important that after the recruiting experience is over the player thank the coach for assistance and perhaps send a thank-you note to show appreciation. A thank-you is in order even if a player fails to be recruited and no team offers a scholarship, or if only a team low on the player's list of choices offers a scholarship. Players must leave their coaches feeling good about the recruiting experience so that future players can expect the same help and cooperation that their predecessors received.

7

THE CAMPUS VISIT

When high school student-athletes visit college campuses, they should not be misled by the way some coaches smile all the time. There are few coaches who truly like to recruit.

"The season itself, the strategy of preparing week-to-week, the mental approach to your team [and] the actual coaching are a lot of fun," says Bo Schembechler, the legendary Michigan football coach. "The difficulty is the tremendous overemphasis on recruiting. Since the media got involved in recruiting, that particular time has become difficult for all coaches. The coach who tells you he loves recruiting is not telling you the truth."

Schembechler says that he loves to coach and work with young people, but he hates the fact that recruiting makes him "an absentee coach" much of the year. "From December to February, recruiting keeps you away from your players and it hurts you," admits Schembechler. "You always have to come back and straighten out problems created the last three months."

Schembechler has a solution he'd like the NCAA to

consider. "What I'd prefer, so that I can do a better job with the players I already have, is for the NCAA to say that coaches in Division I football cannot recruit off the campus." But he is not so naïve as to think that other coaches will allow Bo to have his way.

Schembechler is one of several coaches who have a decided advantage when recruits come to their campus. Not only is Ann Arbor arguably one of the most desirable college towns to live in for four or five years, but few recruits can resist the tradition they find when they get to Michigan. Add to that the fact that the Wolverines are always on national television, always in bowl games, and never on probation, and what you've got is intense competition for scholarships at Michigan.

Make no mistake about it: Visits to three colleges of choice can be the high point of the whole recruiting experience for an athlete, if done properly. The first order of business is for athletes to be as ethical as they hope their future coaches will be. They should never waste a coaching staff's time by booking visitations if they have no intention of attending a particular institution. Colleges in California, Hawaii, and Florida are often victimized by high school athletes who are looking for a sightseeing trip, not a college that they are eager to attend. Needless to say, these vacationers are easily detected and leave a bad impression in their wake.

Believe it or not, the most important part of a campus visit is the preparation work that athletes must do before they arrive on campus. An athlete who arrives at a college and spends the entire time with only the coaching staff, players, and a host or hostess has not made the best use of the visit. A four- or five-year commitment to a college is a major decision, and an athlete must see as much of campus life as can be crammed into a few days to make a wise, informed choice. The student must regard the trip as primarily work—the athlete's college research as it were—to help him or her rank all those schools willing to offer a scholarship.

One high school coach recommends that all visitations be made at a time when athletes are not actually participating in a sport—either their main sport or a secondary one. [1] Athletes should also pick times when they are going to miss a minimum of schoolwork. Making a visit at the expense of missing an important examination is foolish. Athletes who insist on seeing too many schools—or the right schools at the wrong time—run a real risk of being ineligible at the end of their senior year. Even the blue-chipper who is able to court a dozen or more schools should accept four or five visits at the most. Going to too many schools usually clouds the issue, making a clear choice impossible. Such an athlete looks back on all those visits, and everything seems to be one big, blurred experience.

At the same time, an athlete must think hard whether to sign a letter of intent after visiting a college just once or not at all. Players don't have anything to lose by visiting more than one campus.

Basketball superstar J. R. Reid was positive he wanted to sign with the University of Maryland while he was in high school, but his mother insisted that he visit not only Maryland but UCLA, Iowa, and Virginia, too. "I was ready to sign before I left Maryland, but my mother, as wise as she was, said I should wait," Reid told *The Sporting News*. "And she was right. I went to Iowa and felt the same way [that I did about Maryland], that Iowa was the place for me." Finally, however, Reid visited the University of North Carolina and realized that here was where his heart truly belonged, and he went on to enjoy a brilliant career with Coach Dean Smith's Tarheels. [2]

The NCAA allows players to play four years of college ball out of five years as a student (although Duke, Notre Dame, and the service academies try to graduate athletes in four years). In almost all cases, should an athlete decide that the first college choice was wrong and a transfer is necessary, a year of all-important eligibility goes down the toilet. This is why it is crucial that athletes carefully evaluate the school they plan to attend, as well as the coach they wish to play for.

The NCAA has wisely made certain that athletes don't spend too many visits at the same colleges. Prospects formerly could take unlimited trips to the same school, but partly because that practice took students away from their studies and partly because colleges lavishly entertained them, the NCAA placed a limit on visitations. Athletes can now visit an institution only once officially before signing, although unlimited visits are allowed if players foot all the expenses. However, once a recruit signs, unlimited visits are allowed—although once again, good sense should guide all athletes and coaches.

Likewise, good sense should guide a high school student's actions during visitations. If certain misguided coaches suspect that athletes who visit are people of weak moral fabric, they'll take advantage of the fact. An "anything goes" party atmosphere accompanies a high school recruit's visits at all too many schools. Trustees at Southern Methodist University, in the wake of its football scandal that led to the "death penalty," investigated allegations that female students served as paid prostitutes to service recruits.[3]

The recruiting scandals in the Southwestern Conference have become a national joke. The *Tonight Show's* Johnny Carson had this to say about the so-called holy war that television evangelists were conducting against one another in 1987: "What a story—sex, blackmail, payoffs. I thought I was reading about college football in Texas."

No athlete wants to be part of a national joke. Therefore, it is important for all recruits to exercise restraint and good judgment.

Athletes who come from a disadvantaged background must resist the fear they quite normally feel when they first set foot on a campus. With some exceptions, these athletes must realize that they are probably going to rely more heavily on academic-support services than do athletes who come from wealthier families. Northern Arizona University runs a seminar for athletes called Winning in the Classroom, which helps disadvantaged athletes make the adjustment to college life.

"Only four of the twenty-six athletes in the [first] seminar had relatives who had attended college, and many had relatives who were forced to drop out of high school to help support their families," said Lois Stalvey, the seminar's conductor. "Because of this, there could be no real help from home for academic success either in high school or college. As a result, study habits were not developed."[4]

Students should realize that schools put their best feet forward on recruiting visits, using whatever it is that is special about the institution to get letters of intent signed. A mid-size university such as Indiana State shows football recruits its AstroTurf field, noting that in 1966 the Sycamores were the first college team to play a game on an artificial surface. "It never fails to impress recruits," claims Indiana State athletic director Beanie Cooper.[5]

But students must always see things in perspective and spend an equal amount of time inquiring into the school's academic and athletic advantages.

As mentioned, athletes on a visit shouldn't spend an undue amount of time with the athletic department. While still at home, they need to take the opportunity with each recruiter to set up a visit that allows for both unstructured and structured use of time. Unstructured time doesn't mean wasted time. Athletes need to see the campus and the surrounding community. No doubt about it, schools that feel "right" to one person might feel "wrong" or at least uncomfortable to someone else. Black athletes from New York City visiting Clemson University, for example, must determine if they can feel comfortable in the extremely friendly but primarily white confines of a small South Carolina town where the food, people's accents, and landscape will all be unfamiliar. Some black students adjust well and consider the experience a learning opportunity; others feel caged and homesick. Once again, it all boils down to each individual's makeup and expectations.

A player's lifestyle, because it is his or her own, is important. Men who wear a gold earring in one ear, for example, shouldn't play for Memphis State coach Charlie Bailey. *The Sporting News* says he loathes such ostentatiousness. And although non-Mormons are more than welcome to play ball at Brigham Young University, they must give up alcohol, coffee, tea, facial hair, and live-in lovers or else lose their scholarships.

Part of the structured time on a visit should be spent in the student dormitories. There are three basic choices for athletes. Schools such as Alabama and Kentucky believe in putting their student-athletes in dormitories that are principally limited to athletes. These are lavish accommodations, and players really get to know one another, although they tend to stick together and be somewhat detached from the rest of the student body. On the other hand, such dormitory situations provide excellent study-hall facilities, and counselors are readily available.

The second type of housing choice is one in which athletes and nonathletes share dormitory suites. Ohio State coach John Cooper doesn't want an all-football dorm for his athletes. "I think this setup is the best of both worlds," Cooper told Tim May of the *Columbus Dispatch*. "You live on campus, have interaction with the students, but you also become close to your teammates in football." In a typical suite at Ohio State, four scholarship athletes and four nonathletes live together in a high-rise dorm. Ohio State assistant coach Ron Hudson told May, "A big part of education is what goes on outside the classroom, in the interrelationships. When you isolate them, that can get old."[6]

The third situation—much rarer—is when institutions believe in treating athletes no differently from other students, as is the case at Notre Dame. The advantages of such a living arrangement are that athletes really get a taste for college life. And at schools such as Brigham Young, athletes can get a real taste of Provo, Utah, living (if they prefer) by renting apartments off campus.

But although unstructured time is important, each visit must consist of some investigative work. Well before leaving for a college, athletes should ask the school to mail copies of their catalog. Then, either through a college's athletic recruiter or its admissions office, athletes can set up appointments with a number of qualified people to get a real feel for the institution's academic life. Perhaps you will wish to talk to the head of the General Studies program if you are unsure of a major. Or if you have an idea of what to do with your life after college, you would be wise to set up an appointment with a professor or two in the area you are likely to take courses in.

At Ball State University, professors routinely meet with a number of high school students in a given year. They all try to be encouraging but also truthful. For example, if a student comes to see a teacher with questions about journalism, the professor will try to truthfully discuss the rewards and problems associated with such an occupation. After such a meeting, some students seem really charged up about a career in journalism. Others choose another scenario for their lives and seek out a department more compatible with their abilities and dreams.

By talking to a few professors, athletes may be able to determine whether an institution is the best place to spend the next four years. No matter how happy an athlete is on the basketball court or on a lacrosse field, if that individual is miserable in the classroom, the college experience is not going to be a happy one. During that visit, he or she can find out about the school and program's accreditation or lack of it, its strengths and weaknesses, its student-to-faculty ratio (are you more comfortable listening to a lecture with sixteen other students or three hundred students?), the quality of its library, and where its students traditionally find jobs after graduation.

One piece of advice: Unless players are certain that they are utter "rocks" as students, they should not choose the easiest major they can imagine. The best method is to choose something they really want to do after college ends. Many professional people once played college ball. Digger Phelps of Notre Dame takes as much pride in the fact that one of his players became a doctor as he does in knowing that David Rivers made the NBA.

"Gary Nowak is a surgeon," said Digger Phelps. "And I think he's a better doctor because he knew what it was to be 6 and 20 one year, and he knew what it was to be 26 and 3 two years later. You're not going to go through life undefeated, but hopefully, you're not going to go through life losing every game either."

Athletes should be wary of coaches who have no interest whatsoever in their students' academic lives. These are the coaches who won't let you out of a practice when you need to be preparing an important laboratory assignment. Digger Phelps, Bob Knight, Joe Paterno, and Bo Schembechler are winners on and off the field because they are able to make adjustments for an athlete's academic needs.

"I don't want to pat myself on the back, but I never wanted to be just a football coach," said Joe Paterno. "I've always enjoyed the academic environment, and I've always tried to go to things that are taking place on campus. The campus is a fascinating place, and I try to stay involved with the faculty. It's important that the faculty understand that football has a place in the university, and that the tail's not wagging the dog."

In fact, the more times athletes refuse to attend schools because coaches seem insufficiently concerned with academics, the sooner coaches will wake up and adjust their ways. According to *Sports Illustrated*, Florida's Emmitt Smith, holder of the high school record for career touchdowns with 109, rejected Auburn University in favor of the University of Florida because he felt that Tiger coach Pat Dye didn't take academics seriously enough. Ironically, Dye was an excellent student himself at the University of Georgia, and he cares that his students learn. But the public now questions Dye's values because he played running back Brent Fullwood in a bowl game even though the player had skipped most of his classes the previous term.

Finally, the athlete must spend some structured time with the coaching staff and possibly with the athletic director. This is the time to ask really hard questions. If there is a strong possibility that the coach intends to change a recruit's position, let's say, from pitcher to the outfield or from center to power forward, this is the time for an athlete to learn about such decisions. How deep is the team at my position? What is the status of NCAA investigations, if any? What are the chances that the head coach may leave for other employment in the next few years? Is there any possibility that the university may drop this sport?

That last possibility is getting to be more and more of a reality for programs suffering a financial crisis. During your visit to campus, ask the athletic director point-blank if there is any possibility that the college may drop your sport. For example, in 1987 at one institution, the men's baseball and wrestling teams, along with women's swimming and basketball, were dropped. The university claimed it saved $487,000 by the decision.[7]

Prospects should specifically find out (preferably in writing) what are the grade point averages of athletes at the university and, in particular, what the grade point averages are of players on the team they hope to join. These can vary dramatically. For example, the University of Minnesota's basketball team admitted to *The NCAA News* that it had a terrible collective D+ average (1.8 on a 4.0 scale and not one student with a B average) during the 1988–89 winter quarter, while almost all the women's teams did superior work (48 percent with 3.0 averages or higher).

Beware of schools that are reluctant to report such important details as their graduation rates. In fact, recent legislation by Representatives Ed Towns and Tom McMillen and Senator Bill Bradley may end a coach's silence on such important matters if it is passed. "This kind of information is essential for the committed student-athlete to make a reasonable decision about the future," said Senator Bradley, a former Rhodes scholar and basketball star at Princeton, in an article he wrote for the Scripps Howard News Service. "College coaches and college athletics programs must be accountable for the job they do."[8]

As all athletes can see, the visit to campus is an important event. The decision of where to attend college is one of the most important decisions any young person can make. Many colleges try to pull the wool over its athletes' eyes by showing them a spectacular time, which is unrealistic. For example, the University of Nebraska wined and dined an athlete, picking him up in a limousine to take him to the airport and then having him join a party with the state's governor; actress Debra Winger; and football head coach Tom Osborne. "What was a seventeen-year-old football player supposed to say?" the recruit, Aaron Emmanuel, asked *Sports Illustrated*.[9]

Not that there is anything wrong with a coach taking an athlete out for a nice dinner. But the smart athlete will appreciate the coach who not only tries to sell the school but also gives players an accurate idea of what the academic and athletic experience will be there.

When packing for a trip, a student should bear in mind what his or her schedule will be while at a particular school. For the most part, the student should bring comfortable clothing. There is no need to overdress. The athlete who most impresses coaches is the athlete who acts the most natural in all situations. If an elaborate dinner or formal meeting with the university president or a distinguished alumnus is on tap, by all means bring your best outfit. But for almost all other situations, clean but comfortable clothing that you'd wear on an ordinary dinner date is desirable. If you have any doubts beforehand, simply ask your recruiter what is appropriate to pack in your suitcase.

8

MORE THAN ONE OFFER

Even if athletes receive two, three, or ten bona fide scholarship offers, they can still attend only one school. Choosing the right school is a decision that must be made only with utmost care and only by the athlete. Parents, high school coaches, friends, and advisers can recommend their choices of schools, but it is the student who must ultimately live with the decision. Ideally, then, the player must make the choice. Under no circumstance should an athlete feel obligated to a school after making a visit.

At the end of this chapter is a chart that can be photocopied and used to do a comparison of schools. This chart is only a guideline—a sort of map—to help you find your way to the best school for your purposes. It contains both academic and athletic considerations. Students contemplating a school are advised to put all their dreams on hold for a time and to take a thoughtful, honest look at each school in light of all available facts.

Even when all the facts are known, students occasionally make poor decisions. Some who lack the necessary drive and motivation or talent and attend schools that are too athletically or academically demanding, may end up either transferring or dropping out without a degree. Some attend schools without giving sufficient thought to the economic status or racial or religious makeup of the student body, geographical location of the institution, or the personality of the team itself; these may wind up feeling horribly out of place.

Some attend schools because they admire a coach and then turn disgruntled when that coach is fired, retires, or is hired elsewhere. Nonetheless, despite the strong bonding that exists between college athletes and their coaches, the only way a student can follow a departed coach to another institution is to sit out a year and give up a year of eligibility. This rule, surprisingly, isn't the NCAA's. It's a mandate put in by the Collegiate Commissioner's Association.

This rule is particularly irritating because student-athletes, in effect, give up a right that nonathletes enjoy. The Collegiate Commissioner's Association may inadvertently penalize a student for life. For example, say a player comes to Clemson University to study English and finds that what he really wants to do is be a magazine writer. Clemson doesn't offer magazine writing in its curriculum, but the University of South Carolina does. The player then has a difficult situation. Either he must transfer and lose eligibility or stay and play, thereby jeopardizing his future career. It seems a particularly unfair rule, but the chances of its being changed anytime soon seem doubtful. Imagine the uproar if a J. R. Reid were allowed to leave the University of North Carolina for, say, Duke. Or Rodney Peete were allowed to leave Southern California for UCLA? Nonetheless, athletes are players, not slaves, and it is the author's opinion that the NCAA should stand up to the Collegiate Commissioners Association on this one.

Another thing students must decide is whether or not they can afford to attend a particular college. In other words, how much money does it take to survive at a school after the tuition, books, and board fees are paid by a scholarship? Once the academic year begins, athletes cannot accept any part-time employment. The NCAA enforces this rule to prevent coaches and boosters from paying athletes illegally through "phantom" jobs. Unfortunately, the effect is to strip athletes even further of basic rights as citizens.

Although coaches may yank scholarships away from players, it may be difficult for players to get out of a scholarship. Hence, players must seriously consider the consequences when they sign a letter of intent. One of the saddest situations in recent memory occurred in January 1987 when Jacksonville basketball coach Bob Wenzel refused to let his 6-11 center, Jason Cudd, out of his signed commitment. Cudd, who wanted to play for Furman in South Carolina, a college located a short drive from his home, committed suicide. "It sounds awfully callous, but we didn't give him a release because of the way he went about leaving," a shocked Coach Wenzel told *The Sporting News.*

Only after sufficient reflection, therefore, should the student sign a binding letter of intent. The student must have all scholarship offers in writing and should not be shy in the least about protesting if some offer made in person is not what appears in writing. Any offer that is not written down is not legally binding, and the student-athlete should accept no oral promises. Students must also separate their lifelong dreams of starring on a college team from the reality of how each coach plans to use them.

For example, the University of Michigan's head football coach, Bo Schembechler, is not only one of the most persuasive recruiters in the country, he's also an effective recruiter because he recruits "based on need." Unlike Coach Gerry Faust, who has found himself in trouble while coaching football at Notre Dame because he recruited too many players at some positions, not enough at others, Schembechler has a talent for visualizing his needs. But since not all recruiters are Bo Schembechlers, it's up to individual recruits to ask some basic but all-important questions before accepting an offer, such as:

> *How do I fit into the team's plans?*
>
> *Do you plan to use me at the position I played in high school or convert me to another position?*
>
> *Do you plan to use me only on special teams?*
>
> *What other recruits have you signed that play my position?*
>
> *How many junior-college transfer players are on the next roster? Who are they and what positions do they play?*
>
> *What redshirts and roster players also play my position? In other words, who is my main competition?*

Both you and your parents should be of one mind when the final decision is announced. No matter how sure you are that you're attending a certain school, make no announcement to newspaper reporters until both you and your parents sign a letter of intent. For one thing, college coaches have been known to turn fickle at the last minute, withdrawing oral offers to give them to some other prospect. For another, you or your parents may have a change of heart—with embarrassing consequences.

By way of example, consider an El Toro, California, defensive lineman named Scott Spalding. Scott was so certain in January 1987 that the University of Southern

California would be his school, he told the media, "I have USC in my blood."

But in February, he signed instead with USC's arch-rival, UCLA. What happened? "He must have had a trans-fusion," his coach, Bob Johnson, told *USA Today*.[1]

Can a recruit renege on a promise made to a college? Yes, but only at a loss of face and reputation. For example, a 6-8 basketball forward from Detroit, Derrick Groce, signed a letter of intent with Oklahoma State during the early signing period, only to discover that he'd made a mistake. He was fortunate that the Cowboys released him from his commitment without obligating him to sit out a year without playing ball.

Occasionally, a recruit signs a letter of intent and is allowed to reverse that decision on a technicality. Daimon Sweet, a 6-5 basketball guard from Beaumont, Texas, signed a letter of intent with Southern Methodist Univer-sity before scoring the minimum of 700 on his Scholastic Aptitude Test. But because SMU has a rule stating that no one can sign a grant without first scoring 700 on the SAT, Sweet, too, was able to renege on his commitment and later signed a letter of intent with Notre Dame.

Recruits must realize that scholarships today are not guaranteed for four years. Scholarships are hard to come by these days. For example, beginning in 1988, the NCAA limited each institution's football scholarships to twenty-five annually, although the maximum number of sports scholarships permitted is ninety-five. Such a rule seems to penalize the Notre Dames and Brigham Youngs and Dukes who graduate a high percentage of their players. "I could go for the twenty-five if they would just take the ninety-five limit off the other end and reward you for keeping kids in school," groused LaVell Edwards of BYU. If athletes fail to make the team or are injured on the playing field, many coaches yank their financial aid outright or make the athlete feel so guilty or uncomfortable that he or she voluntarily hands it back. Some of the better coaches, including Penn State's Joe Paterno, allow athletes who have been hurt while playing or practicing to finish their degree without giving up their scholarship.

But Paterno and the others are an exception to the rule. Other coaches, such as former Kentucky basketball coach Eddie Sutton, occasionally sign too many scholarship players before spring practice begins, then weed out those players who no longer "deserve" the money. A good idea for athletes is to talk with other players at the school to see how individual coaches handle hurt or cut players as a matter of policy.

Recruits should also know that colleges won't always honor the scholarships in the event that an injury off the field or some other calamity shortens a player's career. One of the more generous gestures made by Ball State basketball coach Rick Majerus occurred in June 1987 when he told 6-10 basketball recruit Thomas Lick that he'd still honor his scholarship after the player lost his left leg in a motorcycle accident.

Now see Chart 2, which athletes should photocopy and then fill out to the best of their knowledge. Only by comparing one school against all other schools can a student-athlete make an intelligent decision about what school to attend.

CHART 2: How To Select A University

Write yes or no or the answer to the particular question asked in all boxes that apply. Leave blank those that do not apply. If you cannot answer a particular question, investigate until you can obtain the correct information. Make as many copies of this form as you have scholarship offers. Do *not* write in this book.

Question	School 1	School 2	School 3
Does the school possess full accreditation?	☐	☐	☐
Is the school considered to be one of the more prestigious research or liberal arts colleges?	☐	☐	☐
Is my choice of major accredited?	☐	☐	☐
If I do not have a major, is the "General Studies" or "Undeclared Major" program known as a quality program?	☐	☐	☐
What is the average number of students in classes that I need to take in my freshman year?	☐	☐	☐
What is the average number of students in classes that I need to take in my declared major?	☐	☐	☐
What is the graduation rate of male athletes at this institution?	☐	☐	☐
Of female athletes?	☐	☐	☐
Of minority athletes?	☐	☐	☐
Of players in my preferred sport?	☐	☐	☐
Has the school been on NCAA probation in the last five years?	☐	☐	☐
Have any of the coaches ever been found guilty of violations by the NCAA?	☐	☐	☐

Question	School 1	School 2	School 3
Are scholarships ever taken away from players who are incapacitated in some way?	☐	☐	☐
If I am a member of a minority, what is the ratio of members of my race to the general student population?	☐	☐	☐
What is the total budget for athletics at this university?	☐	☐	☐
What is the budget for my sport?	☐	☐	☐
What is the condition of facilities, uniforms, and equipment?	☐	☐	☐
How many years remain on my coach's contract?	☐	☐	☐
Is there a fairly good chance that my head coach won't be here in a few years?	☐	☐	☐
Has my coach ever been arrested or involved in a scandal?	☐	☐	☐
How many junior-college players are on the roster?	☐	☐	☐
How safe are the campus and surrounding area?	☐	☐	☐
What free academic-support services are available?	☐	☐	☐
Have athletes been involved in any scandals of any sort in the last five years?	☐	☐	☐
Has a high number of this college's players been injured in competition?	☐	☐	☐
Are any players or coaches in favor of using steroids or illegal drugs?	☐	☐	☐

Question	School 1	School 2	School 3
What specific conflicts have team members had with one another?	☐	☐	☐
What medical services are available at games and practices?	☐	☐	☐
If I didn't have a scholarship, would I attend this college anyway because of its academic offerings?	☐	☐	☐
What sort of non-sports-related jobs have athletes taken after leaving college?	☐	☐	☐
After looking at the depth chart, do I honestly believe I can earn a letter at this institution?	☐	☐	☐
Taking the geographic area into consideration, how much money will I need each year for expenses?	☐	☐	☐
Am I going to this school because someone else wants me to attend it?	☐	☐	☐
Has any recruiter or booster made an improper offer?	☐	☐	☐
Does the personality of the school and the school's team suit me?	☐	☐	☐
Have I talked to			
1. the head coach?	☐	☐	☐
2. an academic counselor?	☐	☐	☐
3. the athletic director?	☐	☐	☐
4. at least 4 or 5 players?	☐	☐	☐
5. 2 or 3 professors in my major?	☐	☐	☐
6. the dorm director?	☐	☐	☐
7. the financial-aid officer?	☐	☐	☐

Question	School 1	School 2	School 3
8. my high school coach?	☐	☐	☐
9. my high school counselor?	☐	☐	☐
10. my parents?	☐	☐	☐
What does this scholarship offer include or lack in comparison to others I've received?	☐	☐	☐
What other recruits have signed or indicated they would sign letters of intent with this school?	☐	☐	☐
What are my SAT and/or ACT scores?	☐	☐	☐
What is the average SAT/ACT score accepted by this school?	☐	☐	☐
What are the best features and worst features of this school, head coach, assistant coaches, area of the country, and academic program?	☐	☐	☐

STRICTLY
FOR MEN

This chapter attempts to discuss several common questions that high school male student-athletes have that did not readily fit into the preceding chapters. In addition to this chapter, readers should turn to Chapter Eleven to get the answers to other questions that apply to both male and female athletes.

Why Should Athletes Play
the Recruiting Game Honestly?

Much of this book has talked about the evils of recruiting perpetrated by coaches, recruiters, and boosters. However, a portion of the blame must be accepted by high school athletes who play the recruiting game with their hands out, looking for any sort of improper or illegal payment they can get.

One of the most unpleasant stories in recent memory involved a high school basketball superstar who visited Indiana University and demanded to know what the players received. When the incredulous players told the recruit that Coach Bob Knight was aboveboard, the jaded athlete told them he didn't believe any program was honest.

The truth be told, many honest coaches have left the coaching business because of similar young men. Former Florida State football coach Don Veller quit his job to coach golf at FSU because recruits so often insulted his integrity by asking him to do illegal things. "One highly regarded player from back East wanted me to pay the expenses for his girlfriend while he was on a visit," said Veller. "I would have liked to have stayed in coaching football if it hadn't been for that."[1]

Current Florida State football coach Bobby Bowden's wife, Ann, says that her husband wants only honest players on his team—and not just those that *look* honest but those who *are* honest.

"The appearance is what you do because that's what people expect of you, but actually being honest is something you have to expect of yourself," said Ann. "You have to do what people expect of you for the outer appearance, but then your own personal conviction has to come from your honesty inside."[2]

In one national incident, a group of football players who accepted improper booster gifts and favors were caught and suffered national disgrace. Texas Christian University football coach Jim Wacker dropped seven players from his team who had taken improper gifts and favors without his knowledge, even though doing so destroyed his team.

In short, it appears to be only a matter of time before the NCAA uses its power to punish players caught in recruiting violations as well as their coaches and schools. Recruits are advised that honesty is the best policy.

What Else Can I Do to
Get Recruiters to Notice Me?

In addition to playing as competitively as possible in high school games, many players increase their value to college scouts by performing well in summer camps sponsored by major universities.

By way of example, 6-5, 250-pound defensive lineman Mike Lustyk of Bellevue, Washington's, Interlake High School, attracted scouts by averaging sixteen tackles and two sacks per game as a senior. But what really sold them were his performances at summer camps sponsored by the University of Washington and the University of Nebraska. As a result, Washington ranked him as its number-one lineman prospect, and he signed with the Huskies.

Since other college coaches, particularly from the Northwest, also attend camps such as the one sponsored by the University of Washington, players who ordinarily might not attract scholarships can demonstrate their talents and rise from obscurity. Such was the case with Bart Hull, son of former National Hockey Leaguer Bobby Hull, who rushed for 1,352 yards and fourteen touchdowns, but whose heroics went unnoticed because he played for a private high school in Vancouver, Canada. "American universities don't scout Canadians unless they're about 300 pounds," the younger Hull told *USA Today*. "I wanted to get into the American system if I could."[3]

Hull's gamble paid off. Boise State coach Skip Hall attended the Washington camp and signed Hull.

Other football players opt to attend five-day recruiting and evaluation camps sponsored by organizations such as Scouting Report, which bills itself as the nation's "largest high school scouting service." The Scouting Report claims to offer instructional skills taught by former college and

NFL coaches, as well as to provide scouting information to college recruiters.

What If I'm Not Recruited?

Athletes who are not recruited may opt to attend lower-division schools under NCAA jurisdiction where the competition is not so fierce. Through a combination of summer jobs, financial aid, and parental financial support, many athletes find it rewarding to participate in intercollegiate competition on a less pressure-filled level.

Another possibility, although risky, of course, is for athletes to pay their own way to a scholarship-granting school and then hope to make the team as a walk-on. Many football teams, for example, are accepting walk-ons now that the NCAA has limited football scholarships to twenty-five annual awards with a ceiling of ninety-five scholarships overall.

Athletes should write to the athletic departments of their choice to find out specific information about the school's walk-on policy. At some universities, including Ball State University's basketball team and Texas A & M's football team, walk-ons are taken as a part of team tradition. Ball State's Sixth-Man Squad, for example, allows five or more players to make the team on a rotating basis. Texas A & M's Twelfth-Man is composed of students who participate in special-team activities.

But every year there are success stories told about nonscholarship players who try out for their college team and wind up starting and even starring.

One of the great success stories in college football is that of Gregg Garrity at Penn State University. No recruiter thought Garrity, only 5-10 and 170 pounds, was worth wasting a scholarship on. But Garrity not only made the team as a walk-on, he finished his career with fifty-eight catches (eighth highest in Nittany Lion history at the time), starred in the 1983 Sugar Bowl, and then fought his way into the National Football League as a starting wide receiver for the Philadelphia Eagles.

Some coaches actively encourage walk-ons. Iowa State football coach Jim Walden once had sixty-six volunteers for special teams and bench strength. "If they can run and chew gum, they can help us in practice and maybe on special teams," Walden told *The Sporting News.* And Kansas State football coach Stan Parrish once tested 175 Wildcat walk-ons when his team lost four of its first five games in 1986.[4] Even former Coach Eddie Sutton at mighty Kentucky resorted to walk-ons when his squad of regulars fell apart for one reason or another.

Football coaches at the University of New Mexico and Mississippi State have even placed ads in their school newspapers in hopes of attracting talented walk-ons. In 1986, Mississippi State coach Rockey Felker added ten walk-ons to his roster, eight of whom had responded to the ad.

Should Athletes Consider
Going into the Service?

One question that many young men have who do not get recruited is whether a career in the armed forces might not be a good decision. One reason to consider entering the service is if a player's high school career was plagued by injuries and he never achieved the performances he and his coach believed him capable of. For some athletes, the service is precisely what they need. If players haven't reached their full growth by their senior year, they may still be a couple of years away from making a college team. In that case, the two to six years spent in the service may be to their advantage.

A University of Minnesota basketball player named Richard Coffey, for example, told *The Sporting News* that he was too scrawny as an Aurora, North Carolina, high school player to be seriously considered by Big Ten recruiters. But after joining the Army's 82nd Airborne Division, Coffey said he "grew five inches and gained about 40 pounds." Upon mustering out, Minnesota offered the 6-6, 220-pound Coffey a scholarship, and by his sophomore year his leadership earned him the title of team captain.[5]

In 1988, *The Sporting News* reported that no less than twenty-four NCAA Division I basketball players listed military service on their records.

What About Turning Professional?

Another question that faces baseball players more than other athletes (but also applies to hockey and soccer players as well as golfers) is whether to attend college on a scholarship or to sign a professional contract. Although this question needs to be addressed by the individual player, it is clear that an increasing number of players are choosing college ball as a way of getting an education while simultaneously receiving valuable coaching (often from former major-league players-turned-coaches such as Wally Moon and Gaylord Perry) as well as playing experience. "College was important to me because it let me experience being independent," Oakland shortstop Walt Weiss told the *San Francisco Chronicle*. "Unless you're a phenom, I can't see signing right away."

In recent years, the level of ability at colleges has become at least as high as that of the poorer minor leagues, and some teams (i.e., Texas, Southern California, Stanford, Arizona State, and Florida State) could even beat a major-league club on the college's best day.

According to *USA Today,* no less than thirty-five of fifty-six players in the 1988 All-Star Game once played baseball in college, including such stars as Dave Winfield (Minnesota), Frank Viola (St. John's University), Vince Coleman (Florida A & M), and Will Clark (Mississippi State). Moreover, twice as many collegians as high school players are now chosen in the annual amateur draft—a complete reversal of what occurred in the late sixties and early seventies.

Only a few clubs, such as Kansas City, still prefer signing high school players. "Our focus is still on high school players so we can bring them into our system and develop them the way we want," Royals general manager John Schuerholz told *USA Today.* "That way you don't have to deprogram a college player and teach him all over again."[6]

Mike Sullivan, a former catcher in the Cincinnati Reds organization and now a competitor in professional lumberjack events, told youngsters that if he ever has a son, he wants him to attend college unless the boy is offered a huge bonus. Sullivan signed for an insignificant amount of money and felt that he had to play despite an injury to his throwing arm because he feared the team would drop him in favor of a high-priced bonus player. "They didn't have enough of a stake in me," said Sullivan.[7]

Players drafted out of high school also need to consider what round they are drafted in by a major-league team. "Let's face it, the odds of making it to the big leagues when you're below a tenth-round choice are astronomical," José Canseco of the Oakland A's, himself an exception to the rule as a fifteenth-round pick, told sportswriter C. W. Nevius.

Even if a player does decide to turn professional out of high school, however, he should try to get something into his contract committing the major-league team to pay the cost of his education during the off-season.

What About Attending
a Junior College?

Perhaps the most common dilemma for high school seniors who fail to meet the requirements of Proposition 48 is whether to attend a junior college or to give up a year of eligibility and sit out a year at a four-year school. This choice may become less difficult as more conferences put limits on the number of Proposition 48 casualties that a university can sign. "We're [the Southeastern Conference] sending a message to high school athletes . . . that we mean business," Vanderbilt athletics director Roy Kramer told the *Atlanta Constitution*. "Gradually, we'll be to a point where we won't make any exceptions; and in the long run, I think we're doing more for young people than by letting them get by just because they are athletes."[8]

Some schools, including the University of Georgia, simply refuse to sign casualties—period. On the other side of the coin, there seems to be growing support for making casualties sit out a year but later restoring the year of lost eligibility.

There are arguments for both sides. Going to the four-year school allows athletes to get better acclimated to the academic demands put upon them during their freshman year. In addition, by associating with players on the team, the athlete is more quickly accepted by his or her peers when the penalty year ends. Unfortunately, practice sessions are forbidden, and some players quickly get rusty or out of shape.

On the other side of the coin, some players prefer to attend junior colleges so they can continue playing ball virtually free of the restrictions that limit playing time at four-year colleges. The eventual success of such players as football's O.J. Simpson and basketball's Anthony (Spud) Webb is testimony enough to the level of competition a player finds on the "juco" circuit. In addition, basketball coaches Billy Tubbs (Oklahoma) and Jerry Tarkanian (Nevada–Las Vegas) particularly like using junior-college players because they themselves once attended two-year schools. And when you consider that many junior colleges now offer scholarships to play, this choice becomes increasingly popular with students who fail to "predict" by scoring less than 700 on the SAT.

JUST FOR WOMEN

For many years, women's sports took a back seat to men's sports, not only in terms of fan support but also in terms of support from university administrations and athletic directors. This is now changing.

Until the mid-1970s, athletic scholarships for women were rarely given. In fact, there were only 200 women's athletic scholarships given out in 1971 in the entire United States.[1] But in 1972, an important bit of legislation passed that brought women's sports out of the Dark Ages and into the modern era. Despite overwhelming NCAA opposition, a clause in the Education Amendments of 1972 (which took effect on July 21, 1975), known popularly as Title IX, lashed out against discrimination against women in athletics: "No person in the United States shall, on the basis of sex, be excluded from participation in, be denied the benefits of, or be subjected to discrimination under any education program or activity receiving Federal financial assistance."

The effects were immediate. More women coaches were hired at salaries equal or at least close to what their male counterparts made. Scholarships were awarded in proportion to the number of female athletes in a program versus the total number of athletes in a program. "Simply, if 35 percent of a university's athletes are women, then 35 percent of its athletic scholarship funds must go to women," wrote author Carolyn Stanek in 1981. "This policy does not imply that 35 percent of the total athletic budget should be set aside for women in this example, however. It's not a matter of equal funding, but a matter of providing *equivalent* opportunities, insuring that each sport has equipment and supplies, adequate facilities, coaching, training services, secretarial services, publicity, recruiting, scheduling, transportation, tutoring services and housing and dining on road trips."[2]

Women's athletics quickly gained momentum and support. "In 1987, then-retiring University of Wisconsin athletic director Elroy Hirsch noted, "Our women's budget started at $35,000 ten years ago. It's just under $2 million now."[3] And the NCAA reports that although the University of Tennessee's entire budget for women's athletics was $20,000 in 1972, in 1988 it was $1.5 million.

Said former Olympian Donna de Verona, a founding member of the Women's Sports Foundation, "Once we had the law known as Title IX, women's sports exploded: 10,000 women a year attend college on athletic scholarships. Forty-nine percent of our 1984 female Olympians who attended college did so on athletic scholarships, including Evelyn Ashford, Joan Benoit, Tracy Caulkins, and the entire gold-medal-winning basketball team."[4]

And ironically, because salaries for women's basketball coaches escalated so rapidly, an alarming trend started. *The NCAA News* reported in 1988 that a study by two Brooklyn College researchers revealed that men now outnumber women in women's basketball coaching ranks. Although 90 percent of all women's teams in 1972 were coached by women, researchers Vivian Acosta and Linda Jean Carpenter found that only 48 percent are coached by women today. "We've grown so fast, there aren't enough experienced people to get the positions," Nancy Rowe, Plymouth State College basketball coach, told *The NCAA News.*

But the full success of Title IX was short-lived. The U.S. Supreme Court, in the so-called *Grove City* decision, ruled against women's athletics in 1983, stating that "women athletes no longer have the full protection of the Title IX law that prohibits discrimination against women."[5]

As a result of that ruling, in recent years, women's sports once again have felt the financial ax. The *New York Times* reported that nationally, women's sports receive only 20 percent of the total athletics dollar and only 32 percent of total scholarship funds. Moreover, unless the trend is reversed, it appears that future cost-cutting measures by NCAA institutions will continue to weaken women's programs.

"Since men already enjoy a 2–1 advantage [twice as many men receive scholarships as women], it seems unbelievable to me that women are being cut more than the men," complained Christine Grant, the University of Iowa women's athletic director.[6]

Nonetheless, women's sports are coming under increasing criticism from those who believe that the public is interested only in men's sports. "I think it makes small sense to offer scholarships to women athletes," wrote writer Phil Musick in *USA Today.* "To the nay-sayers among you, I would pose a question: Who won the women's field hockey title this year? Or any year you'd care to name? Lacrosse? Synchronized swimming? You get the idea. The equation is as simple as it is obvious. Men's football and basketball constitute the horse; all other sports, including all of those in which women participate, ride in the wagon. . . . The only people who give a hoot about collegiate women's sports are the participants and their immediate families."[7]

Fortunately, an editorial in the same issue of *USA Today* as the above column came to the defense of women's athletics, saying it is ludicrous for critics to maintain that women's sports lack fan support. "Women's basketball games at the University of Iowa and in schools in Texas and Tennessee regularly draw thousands of fans," said the editorial writer. "Universities and colleges should be making it easier for women to share the benefits of athletic competition, not harder. And they should do it because it's the right thing to do, not because they're bound by law. Six times more young women are competing in high school sports than in 1972. Does the NCAA want to tell them colleges respect fairness only when they can afford it?"[8]

The future of women's sports is unquestionably under a cloud, but there is little chance that women's sports programs at colleges will ever decline back to the days before Title IX. *The NCAA News* reports that although the average number of sports sponsored for men declines slightly each year, the average number of women's sports increases slightly. There is real restlessness among women's sports administrators and evidence that the battle against the NCAA will intensify during the 1990s.

"Those of us who have been kicking around women's athletics for twenty-five years don't want to wait until our retirement to see women's athletics achieve equality," Merrily Dean Baker, the former University of Minnesota's women's athletic director (now an NCAA administrator) told the *Des Moines Register.* "After 25 years anyone's patience would wear thin. There has been progress, but just not enough. I see a very real and dramatic change coming for college athletics over the next five to ten years."[9]

Women's athletics may have been dealt a serious blow during the early 1980s when the membership of the Association for Intercollegiate Athletics for Women [AIAW] decided to scrap the association in favor of membership in the NCAA. The perception is that the NCAA does not have the interest of its total membership—that is, its female membership—at heart.

"If only we had some sort of idea of how it would be now if we had kept the AIAW," said former Drake University basketball coach Carole Baumgarten in an interview with the *Des Moines Register.* "The younger women were in support of going with the NCAA, and they reaped the benefits. At the same time, I don't think any sport except basketball has seen any benefit. The other sports have declined except at schools with money. Overall, there have been great losses in other sports since we joined with the NCAA. Those other sports don't have nearly the support they once had from the AIAW."[10]

Dr. Dorothy Harris of Penn State University is a staunch supporter of women's sports as a character-building device. "Women have been traditionally socialized to use their bodies to please others, and males use their bodies to please themselves," said Harris. "Through physical activity, exercise and sports, women discover they too can use their bodies to please themselves.

"They become integrated and discover they too can use their bodies for mastery and competence, for joy, for disappointment, for whatever. That doesn't happen in any other avenue except sport."[11]

One very important difference between men's and women's athletics is that, by and large, women's recruiting has been largely free of scandal. Although the same full scholarships available to men are available to women, offers of automobiles and large signing bonuses for female athletes are only occasionally reported. Nonetheless, there isn't a single women's basketball coach who will say that he or she has never heard of a flagrant violation committed by a competitor. In addition, because athletic budgets are now numbered in the millions instead of the thousands, pressure on athletes and coaches has increased manyfold.

Nearly all the information contained in this book is of use to female athletes. They sign the same letter of intent that male athletes do, and they are bound by the same NCAA regulations, including adherence to Proposition 48.

11

TEN COMMANDMENTS FOR RECRUITS

The horror stories involving payoffs to athletes are similar every year. The only thing that really changes is the names of the athletes. But one difficulty for high school seniors is that even with recent improvements, the *NCAA Manual* is still not an easy book to read and understand. The intent of this chapter is to outline some of the things that every recruit needs to know. If an athlete has any doubt whatsoever about NCAA procedures, the best bet is to consult his or her high school coach or to contact the NCAA itself. All the information below is adapted from the *NCAA Manual*.

First Commandment: Thou shalt ask your coach exactly how many in-person contacts a recruiter for your sport is allowed to have with you AT HOME and AT YOUR HIGH SCHOOL.

Second Commandment: Thou shalt receive no extra benefits (not even a school cap or a button) from a recruiter that aren't given to nonathletes. This includes clothing, meals, transportation, loans, cars, clothing, and favors for relatives.

Third Commandment: Thou shalt know exactly how long athletes in your particular sport can stay at a college on an official visit and what the NCAA allows the university to pay for.

Fourth Commandment: Thou shalt not announce what school you plan to sign with until you and your parent/guardian are ready to put your signature on a letter of intent. Thou shalt read every line of the letter of intent and not sign it until the university provides you with a letter verifying the amount of your athletic financial aid.

Fifth Commandment: Thou shalt not sign any contract with a professional sports agent or professional team (without written NCAA approval for athletes who are amateurs in one sport, professionals in another), nor should you accept any money or gifts from either, at the risk of losing collegiate eligibility.

Sixth Commandment: Thou shalt not take a part-time job during the regular school year.

Seventh Commandment: Thou shalt not participate in any all-star game without the specific approval of the high school athletics association that governs at the state level.

Eighth Commandment: Thou shalt not accept free tuition or a reduced rate at a specialized sports camp run by an NCAA institution.

Ninth Commandment: On an official visit to a school, thou shalt not ask the school to pay for the meals of anyone other than two parents or two guardians. The NCAA permits the school to pay parental expenses only one time.

Tenth Commandment: On an official visit to the school, thou shalt accept only entertainment comparable to that of normal student life and not excessive in any way.

SCHOOLS FOR SCANDAL

This list contains the names of many institutions that have run afoul of the NCAA in recent years. Why print these names? So that athletes can closely question these recruiters, particularly those that could face the NCAA's "death penalty" if hit with additional serious infractions. In addition, even if a particular athlete is honest, he or she acquires a certain limited guilt-by-association by joining a team that the public has come to think of as a chronic cheater.

At one time, the Southwestern Conference had no less than four member schools on NCAA probation—including Texas, Texas Christian, Southern Methodist, and Texas Tech. In 1985, *The Sporting News*'s Joe Marcin attacked the NCAA for its policy of secrecy regarding schools in danger of receiving the death penalty and named these schools as prime suspects: Akron, Arizona, Arizona State, Clemson, Colorado, Florida, Illinois, Kansas, New Mexico, Oregon, Southern California, Southern Methodist, Southern Mississippi, Tennessee State, UCLA, Wichita State, and Wisconsin.

The only way cheating will stop is if recruits refuse to cooperate with cheaters. "How can we improve the recruiting system?" Florida State's Bobby Bowden was asked in the *New York Times.* "Each university president should insist that coaches not violate rules and should make it clear that they will be dismissed if they do. . . . I believe it is the head coach's responsibility to insist on a clean program. He must pass a don't cheat edict to his coaching staff, and they must transmit it to boosters. What do other professions do with colleagues who cheat? Doctors and lawyers have their licenses revoked. The coaching profession should do the same. Coaches should report chronic cheaters to the NCAA."[1]

Richard D. Schultz, executive director of the NCAA, told the *Kansas City Star* that ethics in recruiting is everybody's business. "I was in [the coaching] business for 25 years. . . . Maybe if I had cheated as a coach I would have been a little more successful," said Schultz. "But I think as a coach, you've got to live with yourself first. And the first time you offer an athlete something you shouldn't, you are no longer recruiting an athlete, you're buying a witness."[2]

To be sure, not all schools or coaches continue to cheat after they are caught. Even Southern Methodist University, whose flagrant violations earned the school the NCAA's death penalty, seems intent on cleaning up its collective act. Nonetheless, new head coach Forrest Gregg told the *Dallas Morning News* that he realizes that the road to redemption is at least as long as the road to destruction. "SMU credibility won't come back simply because you say you won't cheat anymore," said Gregg. "Only after a period of time will people realize what kind of program we run. It won't happen with a snap of the finger."[3]

Recruits should know that the NCAA casts a particularly cold eye on programs that have once been on probation, David Berst, the NCAA director of enforcement told the *Dallas Times Herald*. "If you've been involved in violations of NCAA legislation, and information is obtained concerning a possible reoccurrence . . . we're going to want to know if anything's wrong. Once [a college has] been through the process, particularly a significant case, there's no excuse for being involved in serious violations again."[4]

Here are some of the programs that have been in trouble with the NCAA in recent years:

Alabama A & M University. The NCAA discovered that the men's soccer team exceeded the allowable number of scholarship players on the roster. As of October 1988, the school was still not allowed to participate in postseason competition.

Arizona State. According to *The NCAA News,* the Pacific-10 Conference put the track program on probation for two years for eleven rules violations by Coach Clyde Duncan, who was dismissed by the university. During the 1988–89 season, the track team was not permitted to compete off campus. This was the third time since 1981 that serious irregularities, such as improper paying of athletes for personal travel, occurred.

Brooklyn College. In 1987, the NCAA placed this New York City college on probation for one year, among other penalties, for recruiting violations and for maintaining inadequate institutional control.

Cleveland State. Effective April 19, 1988, Cleveland State went on probation for three years and lost the right to play in postseason competition through 1990. According to *The NCAA News,* the university improperly gave benefits to a prospect and a companion from Sudan in hopes of luring a 7-6 basketball player from that country to Cleveland State.

East Carolina. The football program went on one year's probation in 1986 for violations committed under then-head coach Ed Emory.

East Tennessee State. The NCAA in 1986 found that members of the college's basketball staff paid both recruits and varsity athletes. The penalties: forfeiture of two scholarships for one season and the loss of the right to participate in postseason play in 1987.

Eastern Washington University. Because of improper recruiting by the men's basketball team that resulted in the firing of its head coach, Eastern went on NCAA probation for two years (ending in December 1989).

Idaho State. In 1985, the NCAA found Idaho State guilty of violations and imposed a two-year probation on the team. Idaho State was guilty of offering recruits improper inducements and improper automobile transportation. Idaho State also did not properly conduct its practices and tryouts during the off-season.

Iowa State University. Went off probation in December 1988 after suffering a loss of scholarships as a result of an 1986 NCAA investigation.

Louisiana State University. The NCAA hit LSU with a dozen violations in its basketball and football programs in 1986. Sanctions lasting one year were levied against the school. Recruits and their families had received such improper perks as unauthorized automobile transportation, free football tickets, and free meals.

Marist College. The men's basketball program was found guilty of improper recruiting of foreign players. The NCAA placed the school on probation from September 1987 to September 1989.

McNeese State University. Six boosters were forbidden contact with players after being found guilty of improper recruiting. The school's probation ended in February 1989.

Mississippi State. In 1986, the NCAA charged the school with allowing athletes to make improper long-distance calls on school phones. One year probation was imposed.

Oklahoma State University. The NCAA ruled that OSU would undergo four years of probation beginning in January 1989. Penalties include a loss of football bowl appearances for three years and television appearances for two years. The NCAA found the Cowboys guilty of forty recruiting violations. One more infraction in a five-year period would certainly mean the NCAA would impose its "death penalty" on OSU.

Southern Methodist University. The NCAA imposed its severest sanctions on SMU in August 1985 after finding the school guilty of flagrant recruiting and rules violations for the second time within a five-year period. SMU was stripped of its right to play other NCAA schools in 1987, plus it suffered a loss of numerous scholarships and the right to play in postseason competition in 1988. Probation extends until September of 1990.

Texas A & M. In 1988, for giving improper recruiting inducements or the promise of them in football, A & M suffered the loss of 1988 postseason play, as well as a loss of ten recruiting visits and five scholarships in 1988. "I never told you that we were pure," said Coach Jackie Sherrill (who resigned), admitting guilt on four charges.

Texas Christian University. In 1986, despite football coach Jim Wacker's attempt to mitigate the consequences by dismissing seven players who accepted improper payments from boosters, the NCAA hit TCU with stiff penalties. Jim Wacker volunteered information that as many as twenty-nine current and former football players accepted payments from alumni. In addition to forfeiting $343,203 in projected television revenues, TCU suffered probation until 1989.

Texas Tech. The Red Raiders suffered a loss of scholarships in 1987 for one year after the NCAA learned that at least one recruit received money and fancy boots made of ostrich skin. Tech lost three scholarships during the 1988–89 season.

The University of California. Golden Bears officials turned in their program to the NCAA after discovering that a former assistant coach helped a student falsify a transcript. The coach has since resigned and the player dropped out of school. The university forfeited two scholarships during the 1988–89 school year.

University of California at Los Angeles. UCLA lost two basketball scholarships during the 1988–89 season because of violations concerning recruitment and improper transportation of athletes.

University·of Cincinnati. The NCAA imposed probation for three years in 1988 for providing football and basketball players with improper entertainment, inducements, and financial assistance.

University of Houston. In 1987, former head football coach Bill Yeomans admitted giving players sums of cash. The *Houston Post* charged that those amounts totaled several thousand dollars and involved as much as $500 per player.

University of Kansas. The 1988 national championship basketball program suffered three years probation for providing improper transportation and financial assistance to players. The guilty head coach, Larry Brown, had already signed a multimillion-dollar professional contract when the NCAA imposed sanctions.

University of Illinois. In 1988, the school's football program was placed on probation by the NCAA for one year because of violations that occurred under former coach Mike White.

University of Kentucky. The Wildcats' basketball program is now defending itself against seventeen NCAA allegations. Kentucky already was in violation for failure to cooperate fully with a prior NCAA investigation of the basketball program.

University of Minnesota. The men's basketball program was found guilty of giving improper benefits to team members. In addition to other penalties, Minnesota went on probation from March 1988 to March 1990.

University of Mississippi. Recruiting violations committed by the football team, among other charges, caused Ole Miss to be put on a two-year probation that ended in December 1988.

University of Oklahoma. The football program was hit with three years of probation by the NCAA for providing extra benefits and improper assistance to players and recruits.

University of South Carolina. The NCAA placed South Carolina on probation in 1987 for two years, condemning what *The Sporting News* referred to as "a well-organized and well-executed scheme for the sale at face value of basketball players' complimentary tickets." The NCAA found the Gamecocks guilty of giving improper benefits to basketball players. The school came off a two-year probation in March 1989.

University of Southern California. In 1986, USC was found guilty of violating thirty NCAA rules. The football team suffered a loss of seven scholarships from 1986 to 1988.

University of Texas. In 1987 Texas suffered reductions in scholarships and in allowable on-campus visits after receiving two years' probation (later reduced by the NCAA) for what the NCAA termed "serious but not major" recruiting and ticket-selling improprieties. The penalties were light considering that the *Dallas Morning News* had said it interviewed eleven players who admitted receiving up to $10,000 while playing for Texas.

University of Texas at El Paso. Both the men's and women's cross-country and track programs were found guilty of recruiting violations and unethical conduct. The serious nature of the offenses earned El Paso three years' probation, from June 1986 to June 1989.

University of Wisconsin. Wisconsin has had four major violations since 1982, the latest involving an improper $3,100 auto loan from boosters to a star basketball player,

Cory Blackwell. Wisconsin also forfeited twenty-two wins in which Blackwell had participated from (1982 to 1984).

Virginia [Tech] Polytechnic Institute and State University. The NCAA charged Tech with violations in both its football and basketball programs. The school was put on probation until November 1989. The basketball team was barred from postseason play for two years (1987–89). The football team, guilty of awarding too many scholarships under then-coach Bill Dooley, was given a maximum number of eighty-five scholarships through 1990.

West Texas State. The NCAA in 1988 imposed three years probation on State for providing improper financial assistance and benefits to its basketball players.

NOTES

Chapter One

1. This quotation and all others with Bo Schembechler (unless otherwise acknowledged) are taken from a personal interview with Hank Nuwer for the October 1985 issue of *Ozark* magazine.
2. *The Sporting News,* May 4, 1987, p. 17.
3. Tony Barnhart, "Recruiting: The Biggest Game of All," *Don Heinrich's College Football '88,* p. 8.
4. This quotation and all others by Joe Paterno in this book (unless otherwise acknowledged) are taken from Hank Nuwer's interview with Paterno, which appeared in the December 1985 *Inside Sports,* pp. 18–22.
5. *The Sporting News,* April 4, 1988, p. 29.
6. *The Sporting News,* June 17, 1985, p. 49.
7. *The Sporting News,* March 30, 1987, p. 43.
8. *The Sporting News,* September 2, 1985, p. 44.
9. *The Sporting News,* July 27, 1987, p. 40.
10. *The Sporting News,* June 16, 1986, p. 49.
11. *The Sporting News,* March 2, 1987, p. 62.
12. *The Sporting News,* July 1, 1985, p. 43.
13. This quotation and all others in this book are taken from Hank Nuwer's interview with Frank Remington, which appeared in the July 1985 issue of *Satellite Orbit,* pp. 58–64.
14. *The Sporting News,* May 4, 1987, p. 15.

Chapter Two

1. *USA Today*, Feb. 18, 1987, p. 3C.
2. This quotation and all others with Digger Phelps (unless otherwise acknowledged) are taken from a personal interview with Hank Nuwer for the February 1986 issue of *Ozark* magazine.
3. Edward S. Jordan, "Buying Football Victories," *Collier* (November 25, 1905), pp. 21–22.
4. *The Sporting News*, February 23, 1987, p. 16.
5. *The Sporting News*, December 2, 1985, p. 8.
6. *The Sporting News*, May 26, 1986, p. 7.
7. *The Sporting News*, January 20, 1986, p. 34.
8. *The Sporting News*, April 21, 1986, p. 37.
9. *The Sporting News*, May 9, 1988, p. 49.
10. *Rocky Mountain News*, August 21, 1988, pp. 12–13S.
11. R. LaVell Edwards, *Football Recruiting: A Comparison of the Brigham Young University Recruiting Program with a Standard Established from Schools of the College Football Association.* (Ed.D. dissertation, Provo, Utah: Brigham Young University, 1978), p. 40.
12. *The Sporting News*, August 22, 1988, p. 37.
13. *The Sporting News*, April 13, 1987, p. 42.
14. Edward B. Fiske, *Selective Guide to Colleges: 1984–85* (New York: Times Books, 1983), p. ix.
15. Ibid.
16. This quotation and all others with Jeffrey Marx (unless otherwise acknowledged) are taken from a personal interview with Hank Nuwer for the January 1989 issue of *Sport* magazine.
17. *The Sporting News*, February 29, 1988, p. 33.
18. *The Chronicle of Higher Education*, November 23, 1988, p. A–29.
19. Ibid.

Chapter Three

1. Meggyesy, Dave, *Out of Their League* (New York: Paperback Library, 1971), p. 83.
2. *The Sporting News*, October 26, 1987, p. 43.
3. *USA Today*, February 18, 1987, p. 13C.
4. *The Sporting News*, August 19, 1985, p. 42.
5. Ibid.
6. *The Sporting News*, March 23, 1987, p. 19.
7. John F. Rooney, Jr., *The Recruiting Game* (Lincoln: University of Nebraska Press, 1987), p. xvi.
8. *USA Today*, February 18, 1987, p. 2C.

9. Ibid.
10. This quotation and others with Billy Tubbs (unless otherwise acknowledged) are taken from Hank Nuwer's interview with Tubbs which appeared in the December 1988 issue of *Sport* magazine, pp. 72–75.

Chapter Four

1. Kenneth Denlinger and Leonard Shapiro, *Athletes for Sale* (New York: Thomas Y. Crowell, 1975), p. 3.
2. Ibid.
3. *USA Today,* April 13, 1988, p. 13C.
4. *The NCAA News,* March 30, 1988, p. 4.
5. *Rocky Mountain News,* August 21, 1988, p. 1–S.
6. *The Sporting News,* April 7, 1986, p. 20.
7. John Underwood, "Tell Me What You Do," *Sports Illustrated* (September 6, 1976), p. 28.
8. Dan Jenkins, "Pursuit of a Big Blue Chipper," *Sports Illustrated* (September 9, 1968), p. 106.
9. Hickman, Herman, "The College Football Crisis," *Sports Illustrated* (August 6, 1956), p. 7.
10. Ernest L. Boyer, *College* (New York: Harper & Row, 1987).
11. Jenkins, p. 114.
12. This quotation and all others with Bobby Bowden and his wife, Ann Bowden (unless otherwise acknowledged), are taken from a personal interview with Hank Nuwer for the September 1988 issue of *Inside Sports.*
13. This quotation and all others with James Dickey are taken from a personal interview with Hank Nuwer for the January 1989 issue of *Sport.*
14. *The Sporting News,* February 22, 1988, p. 29.
15. *The Sporting News,* June 16, 1986, p. 49.
16. Jenkins, p. 104.
17. Story verified in telephone interview with former Michigan State sports information director Fred Stapely, January 25, 1989.
18. *The Sporting News,* March 23, 1987, p. 19.
19. Ibid.

Chapter Five

1. Bron Bacevich, "The Art of Successful and Satisfying Recruiting," in *Football Coaching,* edited by Dick Herbert (New York: Charles Scribner's Sons, 1981), p. 233.
2. *USA Today,* February 13, 1985, p. 8A.

3. Ibid.
4. *The Sporting News,* June 9, 1986, p. 8.
5. *The Sporting News,* March 2, 1987, p. 62.
6. *USA Today,* February 13, 1985, p. 8A.
7. *USA Today,* February 13, 1985, p. 8A.
8. Bacevich, pp. 234–235.
9. *USA Today,* February 13, 1985, p. 8A.

Chapter Six

1. Bron Bacevich, "The Art of Successful and Satisfying Recruiting," in *Football Coaching,* edited by Dick Herbert (New York: Charles Scribner's Sons, 1981), pp. 231–232.

Chapter Seven

1. Bron Bacevich, "The Art of Successful and Satisfying Recruiting," in *Football Coaching,* edited by Dick Herbert (New York: Scribner, 1981), p. 232.
2. *The Sporting News,* February 29, 1988, p. 5.
3. *The Sporting News,* April 6, 1987, p. 42.
4. *The NCAA News,* April 27, 1988, p. 5.
5. *The Sporting News,* September 21, 1987, p. 57.
6. *The NCAA News,* August 31, 1988, p. 5.
7. *The Sporting News,* September 21, 1987, p. 57.
8. *The NCAA News,* October 3, 1988, p. 4.
9. Douglas S. Looney, "Whatever Happened to the Class of '85?" *Sports Illustrated* (December 5, 1988), p. 106.

Chapter Eight

1. *USA Today,* February 20, 1987, p. 13C.

Chapter Nine

1. Personal interview with Don Veller conducted by Hank Nuwer in 1988.
2. Personal interview with Ann Bowden conducted by Hank Nuwer in 1988.
3. *USA Today,* February 20, 1987, p. 13C.
4. *The Sporting News,* October 20, 1986, p. 53.
5. *The Sporting News,* February 22, 1988, p. 16.
6. *The Sporting News,* July 12, 1988, p. 6C.

7. Personal interview with Mike Sullivan conducted by Hank Nuwer in 1988 for *Country Journal* and *Fireside Companion* magazines.
8. *The NCAA News,* June 22, 1988, p. 5.

Chapter Ten

1. Carolyn Stanek, *The Complete Guide to Women's Athletics* (Chicago: Contemporary Books, 1981), p. 2.
2. Stanek, pp. 30–31.
3. *Chicago Tribune,* June 21, 1987, section 3, p. 10.
4. *USA Today,* June 29, 1987, p. 8A.
5. *USA Today,* June 29, 1987, p. 8A.
6. *Chicago Tribune,* June 21, 1987, section 3, p. 10.
7. *USA Today,* June 29, 1987, p. 8A.
8. Ibid.
9. *The NCAA News,* July 6, 1988, p. 4.
10. Ibid.
11. "Women's Sports and the Media," *Gannett Center Journal,* Vol. 1, no. 2, Fall 1987, p. 66.

Chapter Twelve

1. *The NCAA News,* February 24, 1988, p. 4.
2. *The NCAA News,* July 20, 1988, p. 4.
3. Ibid.
4. *Dallas Times Herald,* June 26, 1983, section C, p. 14.

BIBLIOGRAPHY

Barnhart, Tony. "Recruiting: The Biggest Game of All," *Don Heinrich's College Football '88.*

Benagh, Jim. *Making It to #1.* New York: Harper & Row, 1987.

Bryant, Paul W., and John Underwood. *Bear.* Boston: Little, Brown, 1974.

The Chronicle of Higher Education. September 1987 to November 1988 inclusive.

Denlinger, Ken, and Leonard Shapiro. *Athletes for Sale.* New York: T. Y. Crowell, 1975.

Durso, Joseph. *The Sports Factory.* New York: Quadrangle, 1975.

Edwards, R. LaVell. *Football Recruiting: A Comparison of the Brigham Young University Recruiting Program with a Standard Established from Schools of the College Football Association.* Ed. D. dissertation. Provo, Utah: Brigham Young University, 1978.

Evans, J. Robert. *Blowing the Whistle on Intercollegiate Sports.* Chicago: Nelson-Hall, 1974.

Fiske, Edward B. *Selective Guide to Colleges.* 4th edition. New York: Times Books, 1988.

Herbert, Dick, ed. *Football Coaching.* New York: Scribner, 1981.

Hickman, Herman. "The College Football Crisis," *Sports Illustrated.* August 6, 1956.

Jenkins, Dan. "Pursuit of a Big Blue Chipper," *Sports Illustrated,* September 9, 1968.

Jordan, Edward S. "Buying Football Victories." *Collier's,* November 25, 1905, and December 2, 1988.

Manual of the National Collegiate Athletic Association. Mission, Kansas: NCAA, 1987.

Meggyesy, Dave. *Out of Their League*. New York: Paperback Library, 1971.

Michener, James. *Sports in America*. New York: Random House, 1976.

Morris, Willie. *The Courting of Marcus Dupree*. New York: Doubleday, 1983.

The NCAA News, September 1987 to November 1988 inclusive.

Notre Dame University unpublished biography of basketball coach Digger Phelps, 1985.

Nuwer, Hank. "Call Him Mister Tubbs," *Sport,* December 1988.

_____. "Courting Success," *Ozark,* February 1986.

_____. "Do or Die for the NCAA," *Satellite Orbit,* June 1985.

_____. "Fred Akers: Hooked on Horns," *Inside Sports,* October 1984.

_____. "Joe Paterno: Thinking, Winning and Lasting," *Inside Sports,* December 1985.

_____. Personal interviews for this book with Ann Bowden, James Dickey, Jeffrey Marx, and Don Veller.

_____. "Proving It in Provo," *Inside Sports,* September 1985.

_____. *Strategies of the Great Football Coaches*. New York: Franklin Watts, 1988.

Pitts, Beverley J., Mark N. Popovich, and Anthony T. Bober. "Life After Football: A Survey of Former NFL Players." Unpublished paper sponsored by the National Football League Players Association.

Rawlings, Lenox. "Down and Out in a Basketball Bureaucracy," *Dick Vitale's Basketball '88–'89.*

The Sporting News, January 1984 to November 1988 inclusive.

"Rhymes with Uncanny," *Time,* November 19, 1965.

The Rocky Mountain News, August 21, 1988.

Rooney, John F., Jr. *The Recruiting Game*. Lincoln: University of Nebraska Press, 1987.

Savage, Howard J. *American College Athletics*. Report of the Carnegie Foundation for the Advancement of Teaching. New York: Carnegie Foundation, 1929.

Stanek, Carolyn. *The Complete Guide to Women's College Athletics*. Chicago: Contemporary Books, 1981.

Underwood, John. "Tell What You Do," *Sports Illustrated,* September 6, 1970.

USA Today, May 1987 to November 1988 inclusive.

Vare, Robert. *Buckeye*. New York: Harper's Magazine Press, 1974.

Wolff, Alexander. "The Recruiting File," *Sports Illustrated* (special issue: College Basketball 1986–87).

"Women's Sports and the Media," *Gannett Center Journal.* Vol. 1, No. 2, Fall 1987.

INDEX